The Royal Road to Game Development

using Cocos2d-JS

Candid Publishing.

We think the eco-friendly candid publishing. We make our efforts to fulfill a deep devotion to the contents of the book. And, we strive for reducing materials of the book like paper, ink in order to save our environment. It will be our happy to make the beautiful environment by our small efforts.

The Candid Publisher

considering our Environment.

The source code for this book is available to readers at www.creapple.com
To report errors, please send a note to creapple@gmail.com
For information on getting permission for reprints and excerpts, contact creapple@gmail.com

ISBN-13: 978-1546633655
ISBN-10: 1546633650
1st Edition, May 2017

P·r·e·f·a·c·e

It has been few years from publishing my book 'Enjoy Mathematics, Physics and Games with Cocos2d-JS'. I'd prepared that book for my son and other children because I as a parent want kids to be familiar to boring Mathematics and Physics by funny game. It was happy that my kids and other subscribers gave me positive response on it. One the other had, Some of readers asked me to revise a practical game programming contents rather than Mathematics and Physics. That bring me to write this book.

I would like to write very easy but practical game programming contents in this book. It is my intention to invite real beginner to start game programming. JavaScript is one of the popular programming languages which can be used from mobile to server. That is why I selected Cocos2d-JS for game programming. I believe and hope all reader will get self confidence of programming after following my book step by step. Cocos2d-JS is excellent game framework because it support Cross-platform development. It means you can code one time but you can delopy it to many platform like various web browsers, android, iOS and window mobiles and so on.

I don't want to limit readers to only children, enjoy games. It is my real happy that as many people nurture their own hopes and dreams when they read my book. Children, student, youth even adult, someone couldn't find their own dreams or didn't get a opportunity to find a dream. I hope this book can serve as a momentum to pull out their hidden dreams.

Acknowledgements

I feel hard challenges whenever I try to write a book. It is real happy when I accomplish it. But, it is definitely difficult to overcome lot of obstacles which slow down my writing. It is my objective to provide an efficient way to learn game programming by practical game projects. After many nights of asking myself whether I will get there in the end, the journey is finally at the end. How can I express in words the joy and thanks that I feel at this moment?

To my parents, who have always remained my faithful supporters, to my loving wife and her belief and devotion, and to my son and daughter, who give me courage in hope – I want to speak words of apology before thanks. I ask for forgiveness for my selfish desire to write, which took my time and energy away from family, and as my thanks, promise a happier future.

I also cannot forget the power of knowledge, shared by countless people over the internet. Without them, this book and the sample application will not have been possible. Although I will not be able to see or thank each of them in person, I want to extend my thanks to them as well. I am delighted to be able to contribute what little I can to this pool of knowledge, as they have, through this book.

Finally, I'd like to say thank you to myself as well, for enduring this journey to fulfill a small dream, and to keep a promise to myself.

R·e·s·o·u·r·c·e·s

You can get all sample codes provided in this book. We recommend that you download it directly for reference at the creApple site (http://www.creapple.com). The examples in this book will serve as a useful reference in many ways.

The source code is open for readers to view and use. However, you should note that if the code is reused in another application, the creator's permission must be given separately, and that no responsibility can be taken for the code once reused.

In this book, I've tried to keep independence from a certain software and version. But, it is hard to guarantee backward comparability of Cocos2d-JS framework. I've tested my codes based on Cocos2d-X version 3.15. If you want to know the ways to install programs and set up environment, please visit the creApple site (http://www.creapple.com) and get relevant additional documentations, movie clips which explain it for your references. If there is a change of book content by new software, let me update new instructions and matterials on the creApple site.

In addition, I will provide an on-line lectures at Udemy(https://www.udemy.com) and other channels in relation to game programming and explain about this book.

C·o·n·t·e·n·t·s

β The Ten Commandments of Cocos2d-JS..............73

α

The Ten

Commandments of

JavaScript

I remember that it was my first chance to be ecountered a computer program when I was 11 years old. Displaying the multiplication tables with a computer program and making the famous invader game by myself were almost a shock to me. I still cannot forget the sky I looked up and the excitement I had on my way back home from the first time I put my hands on the computer keyboard.

The young boy naturally made up his mind to learn the computer programming. Having great ambitions, I grabbed the most well known programming book at the time and started to study. It was unclear whether the boy was too enthusiastic or there was no book adequate for his level, but I clearly remember that the book was too difficult.

I hope this book can make 11 year old boy easily acquainted with program. With such hope, I listed up the difficult programming into easy twenty steps. You will not be able to make a computer game right after finishing this chapter, but I believe that you will be able to have enough knowledge on the concept of a program. I arranged the contents in the hopes to nurture the knowledge for a programmer who will be able to make not just a game program but also any programs.

If I could take a time machine like in a movie and deliver this book to myself who was 11 years old, wouldn't it change a lot of things about me now?

1. Antilogarithm

Long time ago, to send a signal from a long distance, they used a torchlight or smoke. They sent signals by keeping one smoke in ordinary times, and adding a smoke each time when there is a sign of a danger.

Computer also expresses various information by turning on and off small electric signals. If electricity flows through a small bulb, it is '1', and if there is no electricity, it is conceived as '0'.

Just a moment here! 1 and 0 do not mean the numbers 1 and 0. 1(On) and 0(Off) only represent the state of a small electricity unit being turned On and Off.

We call one smallest unit of information unit having a value of 1 or 0 as 'Bit'. Remember! Bit is the smallest unit of information in your computer.

With one bit, you can express two states, 0 or 1. Then, how many states can you express with two bits? 0 and 0, 1 and 0, 0 and 1, and 1 and 1, so total of four states can be expressed. As such, when a bit is increased, the number of possibly expressed states increases by twice.

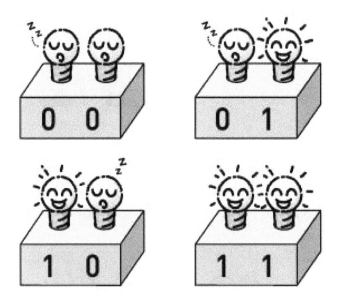

The unit combining 8 bits in one group to express more information is called 'Byte'. In 1 byte, there are 8 bits, so you can express 256 states.

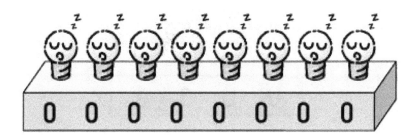

With 1 byte, you can express 256 signals, so if you make promises with each other, you can easily express numbers or English alphabets. For example, you can set the 2nd letter in a byte to represent the number '1', and the 65th letter to represent the alphabet 'A'.

Numbers and English require 1 byte, but to express various letters such as Korean or Chinese, you need at least 2 bytes. We need to agree for a standard that which represents which letter to express all of the various letters with the same meaning. Many are using the representative 'unicode'. ISO(International Organization for Standardization) set the unicode as the standard to express all letters in the world in 1993.

Let us talk about Antilogarithm. It can be easily explained as a unit to count data. I said 'easily', but it is not easy to get the idea right away, isn't it?

Then, let's see the example of the bit we explained above. Bit has two states of being turned on (1) or off (0). The method of expressing a number in two states is called Binary. Since the computer processes the data in the units of bits, so for a computer, binary is the most convenient method.

We are familiar with Decimal, which expresses numbers with 10 cases. While adding 1 each time from 0 to 9, and when 1 is added to 9, one unit is added in front to express unit of 10. When there are 10 of the units of 10, one unit is added to become the unit of 100. Actually, Decimal is very familiar to us, requiring no explanation.

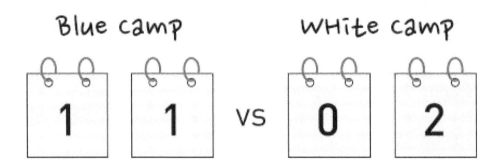

Binary expressing a bit is most convenient for computer, but to express a byte which combines 8 bits, you need more expanded antilogarithm. That is Hexadecimal. With 4 bits, you can express 16 cases. Therefore, to express one byte, which are 8 bits, you need two Hexadecimal numbers.

To express a Hexadecimal, you use numbers 0~9, and alphabets A, B, C, D, E, and F. From 10, it becomes two digit number, so it is expressed with alphabet instead of numbers.

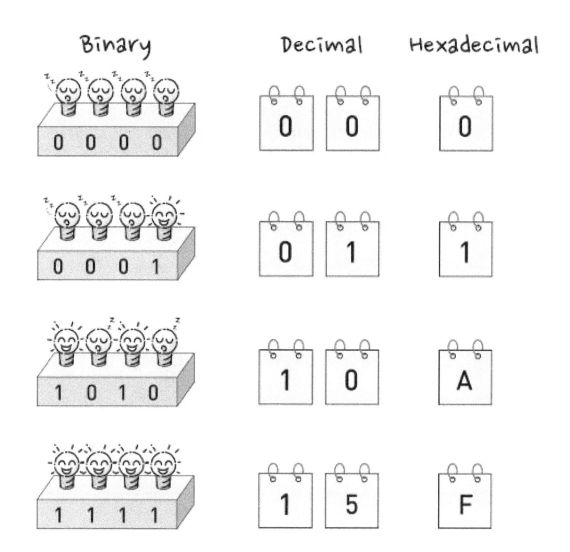

2. Variables

Variables are temporary storage for numbers or letters. You can change the stored numbers or letters as necessary, so it is called a variable.

Let's look at a case of using variables in a game. When you start a game, you start from level 1 and challenge to a higher level. In such case, you make a variable called 'level' showing the level of the game, and when you start the game or every time the level is changed, you store different value here. The score in a game also uses a variable. You make a variable called 'score' and you keep changing the value in this box.

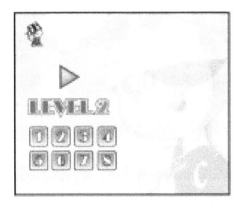 

Let's make a variable. When you make a variable, you need to set the form of data to put in the variable and the name of the variable. The process of deciding the form and name of the variable is called 'Declaring a Variable'. The scores of a game are the forms of integer numbers, so set it as integer type (integer, int), and declare the name of the variable as 'score'. In your JavaScript, regardless of the forms of the variable, write as 'var' and write the name of the variable.

```
var score;
```

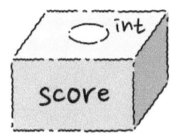

Assigning a value to a variable is called 'Assigning a Value to a Variable'. If you get 10 points in a game, you put integer 10 in the variable score, and if you get 10 more points, you assign the total, 20 points, to the variable.

```
var score;
score = 10;
score = 20;
```

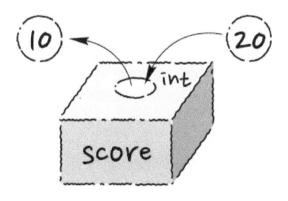

Declaring a variable and assigning a value to the variable at the same time is called 'Initializing a Variable'. When you start a game, the score starts from 0 point. When you declare a variable called score, assign 0 point to the variable to initialize variable score to 0 point.

```
var score = 0;
```

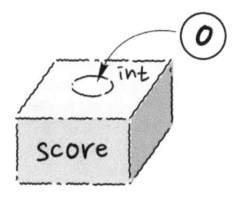

3. Data Types

You learned about variables, so now let's learn about various types of data that can be put into the variables.

In the above, you learned that you need to declare the data type along with the name when you declare a variable. In some programming languages like JavaScript, there are cases that you do not need to declare data types. You, as a programmer, may think it very convenient, but it may cause inconvenience later due to inefficient usage of memory. Ultimately, it means that you need to use data types of adequate size according to the usages of the data.

Data types may vary for each programming language. There are simple data types like Number, String and Boolean types in case of JavaScript. In this chapter, major data types will be explained based on common languages like Java, C and C++ and so on.

The first data type is integer type int that we store numbers without a decimal point. The integer type is the data type that is used to express points or levels as we described in the above when we described variables. The size of integer type is 32 bits, which are 4 bytes.

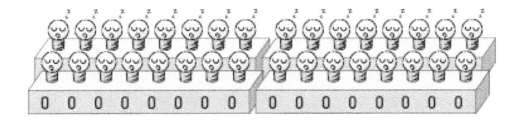

Then, let's declare the levels of a game as a variable called 'level', and initialize it as level 1.

```
var level = 1;
```

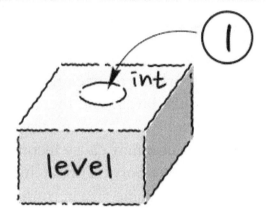

The next data type is a real type float that has a decimal point. The size of the float type is 32 bits, which is 4 bytes. It can naturally express a more detail data with wider range. In languages like Java, real types are subdivided to 32 bit float and 64 bit double.

Then, let's explain real type float with the angle of flying hammer in a game. To express a more detailed movement, it will be better to use a real type that can express below decimal point.

```
var angle = 35.45;
```

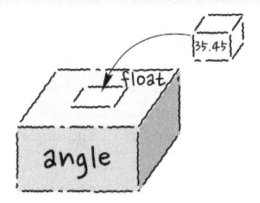

Data types expressing characters are also important. They are divided to Char type which represents a single character and String type which represents a character string.

String type includes the Unicode. As explained above, you can store the letters of different countries using the Unicode.

In our game, we receive input of the names with high scores, and they are displayed in High Score screen. At this time, to receive the names, it is best to use String variable. Let's declare a String variable called name and assign a character string data.

```
var name = "Jonathan";
```

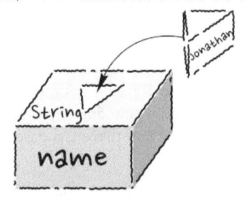

Sometimes, you need to express special characters. They are letters such as back-space or tab, or quotations. To express such special characters, 'Escape Sequence' is used. It may sound grandly, but simply putting a back-slash(\) in front of a character to display, computer recognizes this as a special character. For example, back-space is expressed as \b, tab is expressed as \t, double quotation is expressed as \", and single quotation is expressed as \'.

There are more data types, but let's just look at Boolean data type that represents true and false. It is the data type useful for the cases such as turning on or off the sound of a game. The default value of a Boolean data type is false when the initial value is not declared.

```
var sound = true;
```

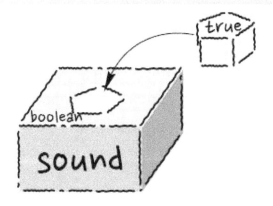

Now you know that there are various types to express data. Once a variable is declared with a data type, most of the cases, you don't change the type. But, there is a case that the data type is changed.

In JavaScript, if a data with different data type other than the declared data type is assigned, the data type is implicitly converted. When you add a number to a string, the string has priority over the number. If you assign a number 5 to the number type variable angle which is a variable previously described as storing the flying angle, then a number 5 is stored in the variable.

var angle = 5;

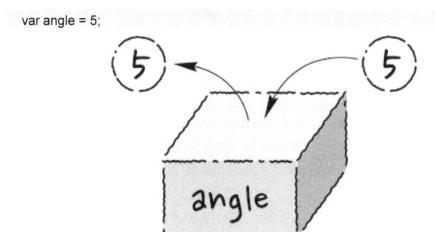

If you add a number 5 to the number 5 stored in the variable angle, what will happen? Both of them are number types, so adding them together will also become the same type. That is, the value of the total of the two numbers, 10, will be stored in the variable.

```
var angle = 5 + 5;
```

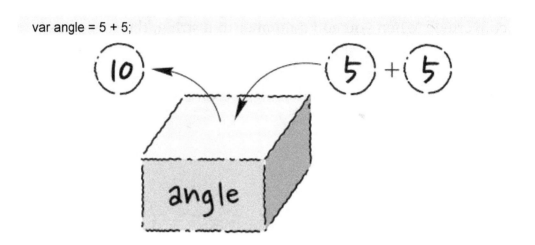

Then, if you add a char type "5" to the number 5 in the variable angle, what will happen? When you add a number type and a char type, it becomes a char type. That is, a string "55", which is the added string of the two values, will be stored in the variable.

```
var angle = 5 + "5";
```

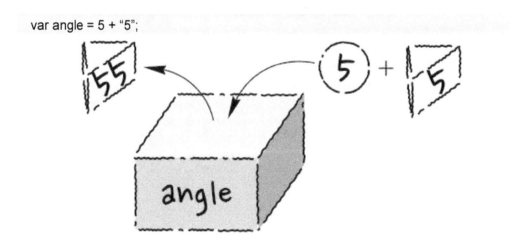

Sometimes, you need a forced type conversion. To change a different data type to a number, you use a function called Number(). If in Number(), if you input a value that cannot be converted to a number, NaN(Not a Number) will be returned.

When you convert the string "55", which you received as a variable named inputString, with Number() function, and input to the variable angle, a number type 55 will be stored.

```
var inputString = "55";

var angle = Number(inputString);
```

Now, let's learn about String() function that converts different type data to a string. When you convert a number 55, which you received as a variable named inputNumber, and input to the variable angle, a string "55" will be stored.

```
var inputNumber = 55;

var angle = String(inputNumber);
```

The function to make Boolean data type that only represents true and false value is Boolean (). Boolean() function returns false only when it has a value of 0, NaN, "", null or undefined value, and it returns true for any other cases.

4. Data Sets

We have learned about various data types like Number, String, Boolean. As you go on programming, there are cases where it is more efficient to combine and manage several data, rather than a single data. As you see in the example of the game, High Score, which shows the names of 5 people with high score, is a good example. For programs playing music, managing the list of songs can be a suitable example.

Array is the representative way to make a data set. Array is a data type specifically for storing sequences of values. Then, let's make an Array named 'names' to store the names of 5 people with high game scores. There are various ways to make an array, and we only know the size of the array, which is 5, and we don't know the names of 5 people to initialize, so let's make the array with the following method.

And, we will put data into the first field that corresponds to No. 1. One thing to remember is that the array always starts from 0, not 1. I also made many mistakes in the beginning, you will be soon familiar with that.

It is easy, isn't it? But, there may be some people asking that isn't it easier to just make and use 5 variables without using an array?

Array provides various functions. Array provides functions to be able to insert or remove components very easily, and provides an easy access to the corresponding position. You can sort the values in an array with a desired standard or change their orders very easily.

```
var names = new Array(5);

names[0] = "Jonathan";
```

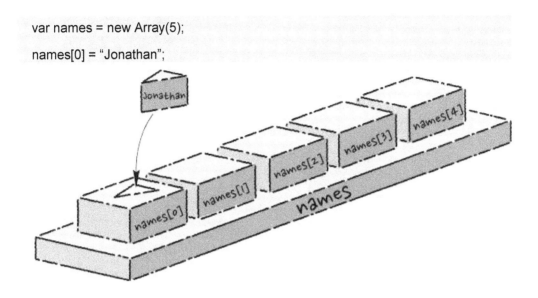

You can also find the number of elements stored in the array easily. Since we set the number of people in High Score in our game to be 5, so the size of the array is not that important, but in a shopping mall program, to get the sum of the prices of the goods in the shopping cart, the number of the goods, which is the size of the array, is very important.

Let's assign the previously input value of the first field of the array to the sting variable highest_name, which means the person with the highest score, and input the size of the array into the integer type variable array_length.

```
var highest_name;

var array_length;

highest_name = names[0];    // Insert the stored value "Jonathan"

array_length = names.length; // Insert the length of array.
```

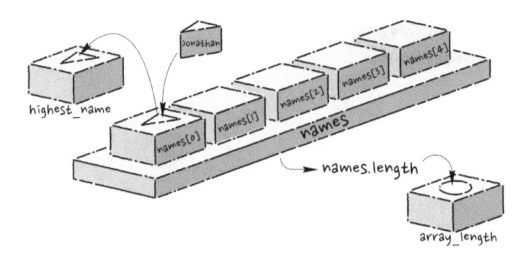

Then, let's talk about our game again. In the screen storing the high scores, we need to show the names of the 5 people with high scores along with their scores. Then, the array shall have a complex 2-dimensional structure, and can we store the names and scores at the same time?

Yes. Such an expanded type array is called multi-dimensional array. Of cause, as necessary, you can increase the dimensions to 3-dimension or 4-dimension, but it is better to use appropriately considering the computer memory efficiency and the level of understanding computers. Usually, 2-dimensional arrays are used most of the cases.

Let's input the name of the person with the highest score and his or her score in the array. Then, if you want to know the name of the person with the highest score, you can look up the data in the position of [0][0], and if you want to know the score, you can look up the data in the position of [0][1].

```
var highscores = new Array();
highscores [0] [0] = "Jonathan";
highscores [0] [1] = "100";
```

```
var highest_name  = highscores [0] [0];  // Insert the stored value "Jonathan".

var highest_score = highscores [0] [1];  // Insert the stored value "100".
```

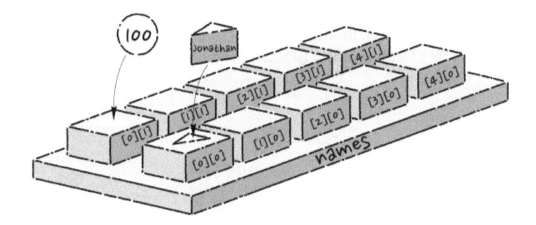

5. Arithmetic Operators

Among the roles of a computer, calculation is the most traditional and still an important function. Among them, arithmetic calculation is a function frequently used in programming.

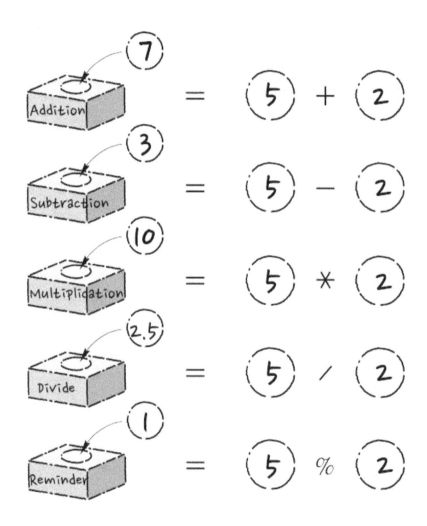

Let's look at the arithmetic operations frequently used in the calculations. From our younger years, we are familiar with the four fundamental arithmetic operations such as additions, subtractions, multiplications, and divisions. Computer is good at the four fundamental arithmetic operations, of course. Not just the four fundamental arithmetic operations, but it also has a calculator that gets the remainder from the division.

Now, let's look at the assignment operator. Actually, an assignment operator is not something special, but it only takes a slightly different form for convenience to use '=' for assignment that we learned previously.

Then, for which occasions is this assignment operator used for? We will look at an example of a game. Game has scores in each level, and it has total scores summing the scores in each level. We will put the scores in each level into a variable named score, and will use an integer type variable named total_score for the total score. Total score will be the sum of the scores acquired from the latest level added to the total score.

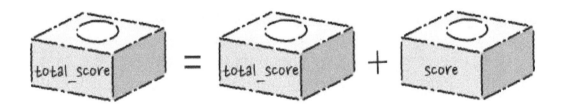

It does not seem comfortable to use total_score repeatedly in the calculation. For convenience, we shall use the assignment operator.

```
var score;
var total_score;
```

```
total_score += score;
```

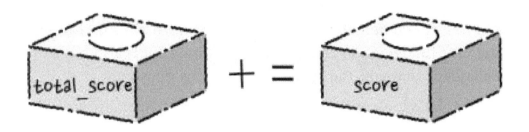

Calculator formula became simpler, isn't it? It is the concept to add the total score by the newly added score. Not only the additions, but you can also use other arithmetic operations you studied above in the form of the assignment operator.

Let me introduce other forms of arithmetic operators. It is the increase/decrease arithmetic operator. Increase/decrease arithmetic operator is used to increase or decrease one by one from a value of a variable.

But, the increase/decrease arithmetic operator has different result when the arithmetic operator is in front and when it is followed. If you want to store the value after the increase/decrease, you use the prefix increase/decrease arithmetic operator, and if you want to store the value before the increase/decrease, you use the postfix increase/decrease arithmetic operator.

It will be easier to explain with an example as well. When we want to count the total number of goods in the shopping basket, we use the prefix increase/decrease arithmetic operator as we count, increase, and store the total number of goods. We will declare an integer type variable after_count which represents the total number of goods and use an integer type variable count to count the number of goods.

```
var score;

var after_count;


count = 0;

after_count = ++ count;
```

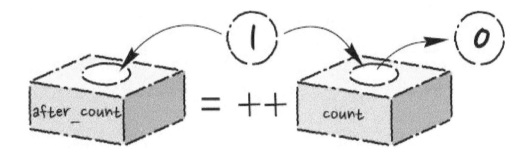

Sometimes, there are cases where we store the value before the increase when we count the numbers. For example, there is a variable to store only the number of male students when we count the number of the students. If there is a female student, we increase the value of the variable COUNT, but we do not increase the variable BEFORE_COUNT. In such case, we use postfix increase/decrease arithmetic operator.

```
var score;

var before_count;


count = 0;

before_count = count++;
```

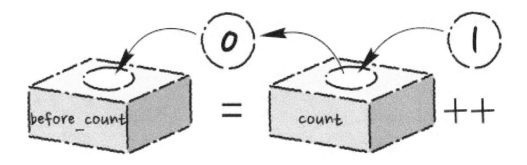

As the calculation becomes more complex, priority becomes more important. Computer performs the calculation based on its own standard, and if we do not know the principles, we may get unwanted result. When we make a program, we always need to have a good habit of making a thorough test scenario, performing a thorough test, and minimizing exceptional cases. Here, let's learn a few important principles of priorities for the calculations necessary for the making of a program.

Let's learn about the two principles of processing when the priorities are the same.

The first principle is carrying out the calculation from left to right.

For the case of operator with the same level as follows, you can carry out the calculation one by one from the left even if there are many variables.

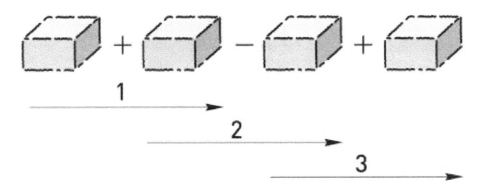

The second principle of assignment when the priorities are the same is for the case of assignment, and in such case, you process from the right to the left, which is the direction of the assignment. You may be confused if you try to memorize the principles, but it is the natural principle if you think it as just an assignment.

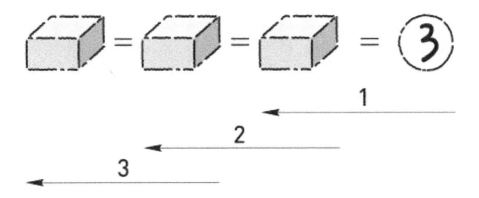

Now, let's look at the important priorities in a calculation. Among the four fundamental arithmetic operations, * and / have higher priorities than + and -.

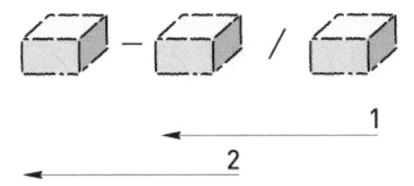

Likewise, in the mathematics that we usually use, multiplications and divisions have higher priorities than additions and subtractions.

Even though that the multiplications and the divisions have higher priorities, if you express additions or subtractions with ( ), it has higher priority. It is a promise with the computer to carry out the contents inside ( ) first.

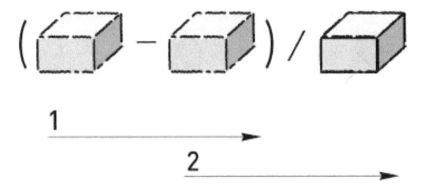

The next priority to learn is the priority for logical arithmetic operator, Boolean type. When you need to carry out a logical decision and assignment, you first perform the logical decision. It seems difficult to set principles, but you will feel it natural when you see the examples.

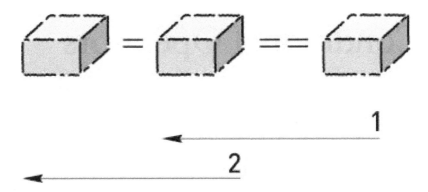

You need to first decide whether it is true or false through the logical arithmetic operation, and then assign the result value to a variable.

6. Conditional Operators

Conditional operators have the roles of determining true and false by comparing the value or figure of a variable. It makes an important decision for the program processing flow that follows. If the condition is not true, it may repeat the processing, or it may skip the corresponding commands.

Then, we will look at the representative conditional operators and their meanings.

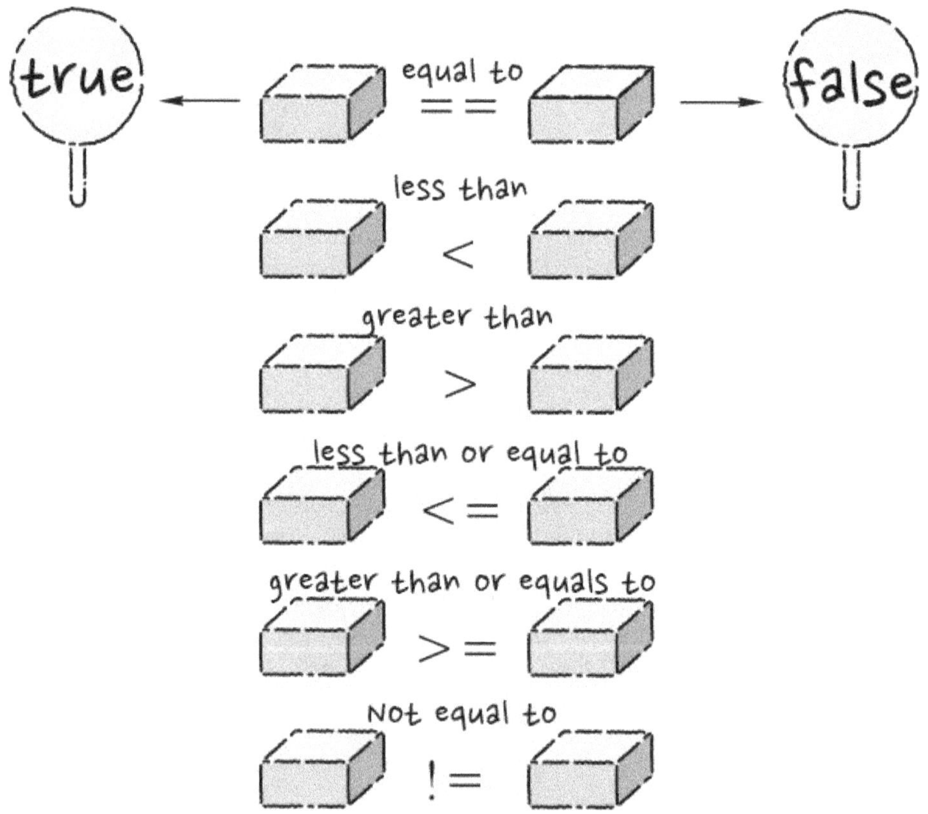

true ← equal to == → false

less than <

greater than >

less than or equal to <=

greater than or equals to >=

Not equal to !=

They are not difficult, aren't they? One thing we need to be careful of is that the symbol '=' we usually use does not have the meaning of equal, but it has the meaning of assignment. To represent the meaning of equal, we use a symbol, '=='.

When there is a value of 2 in the integer type variable value, if you assign 3 to the variable, 3 is stored in the variable. On the other hand, if you compare a variable containing 2 with 3, you get the result of false.

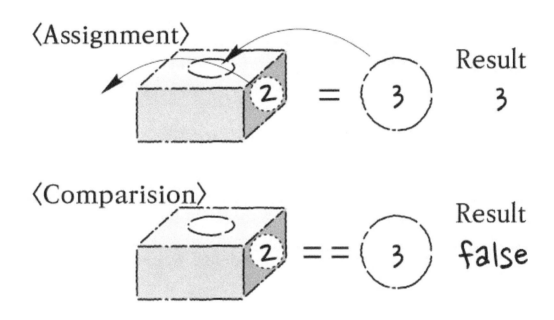

Now, we will show a method to simply process with a conditional formula. There are two results from a conditional formula, true and false. Therefore, you can write as follows for the cases where the conditional formula is true or false.

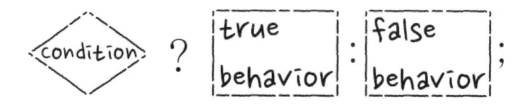

In a game, you can click SOUND button to make it mute or play the sound. In such case, you use a Boolean type variable isSoundOn representing whether the sound state is true or false. If you set the command to turn on the sound as playSound() and the command to turn off the sound as stopSound(), it will be expressed in the program as follows.

```
var isSoundOn;
(isSoundOn) ? playSound() : stopSound();
```

Now let us take a look another type of operators which is Logical operator. Logical operator is the arithmetic operator representing the logical conditions for true and false. It finds true and false of more complex conditions by reviewing several conditions.

Before learning the logical operators, we need to understand the Boolean data type that can represent true and false. The Boolean data type is named after a 19th century English mathematician George Boole. It expresses the result as true or false by the result of a logical thinking process.

Boole suggested a model processing binary information using logical operators, AND, OR, and NOT, in his book 'Laws of Thought' in 1854. It has the basic contents for the logical operators that shall be explained below.

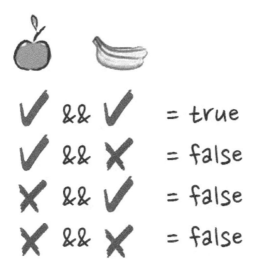

The first logical operator is AND, which shall satisfy both conditions. AND operator uses the symbol '&&'.

Let's think of an example where you have to choose one from apple and banana in a fruit shop. AND operator becomes true only when you buy both apple and banana, and all else becomes false.

Shall we think of the cases where AND operator is needed? In an online shopping mall, to purchase a good, you need to input various informations such as user name, credit card number, address, telephone number, etc. If you incorrectly input any one of those, the transaction shall not be made. You use AND arithmetic operator in such case.

The second operator is OR arithmetic operator that becomes true when only one condition is met. It uses the symbol '||'.

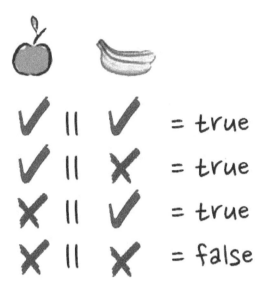

In the fruit shop, if you choose both apple and banana, or if you purchase only one of them, it becomes true in OR arithmetic operator. If you do not choose any one of them, the result will be false.

Where do you use OR arithmetic operator? There are cases where you input interest areas when you register as a member to an online shopping mall. You can choose among several interest areas such as travel, shopping, photograph, sports, etc. If you choose just one among those, it becomes true, and if you don't choose any, it becomes false.

The last logic operator is NOT arithmetic operator. NOT arithmetic operator has the negative meaning of 'is not ~~'. It is expressed with '!' in front, and if the condition follows, it is expressed as '!( )'.

We will use the online shopping mall example as well. Let's think of a case when the user wants to purchase a good, and he or she is not logged in, so a log-in window is popped up. To find out whether the user is logged in or not, we will declare a

Boolean type variable named as isLogIn. We will learn about IF conditional statement later, but let's think of it as a concept of carrying out the following commands when the conditions are met. Let's set the command to display the log-in window as openLogInWindow().

```
var isLogIn;

.........

If ( !isLogIn ) {    // When the value of 'isLogIn' is false, it will be converted to true by NOT operator

  openLogInWindow()

}
```

If the user did not log in before encountering IF conditional statement, the value of isLogIn is false. In such case, by NOT arithmetic operator, the value of !isLogIn becomes true, and it will carry out the conditional formula.

7. Conditional sentence

'If I were a bird, I could fly to you.' It is a sentence that you probably encountered at least once while learning English. Yes. If sentence processes a conditional processing such as 'If it is ~~'. If I were a bird, I will fly to you, and if I were not a bird, I would not be able to do so.

You can simply ask one If condition and process the corresponding contents, but, you can also process for the case which is not so. If I were a bird, I fly to you, and if I were not a bird, I may walk to you. The sentence used for such case is 'If ~ else' sentence.

It is not that difficult, is it? But, even if there is one sentence processing the condition, there may be cases carrying out several commands. So far, you carried out one command, 'flying to you'. But, if I were a bird, you can think of carrying out the command, 'flying to you', the command, 'singing for you', and the command, 'looking into your eyes'. As such, when you process multiple commands, you combine the entire contents to process with '{}' symbol. We call it a block.

Now, let's think of a more complex case. Let's say that there is a case of asking several questions in a row, not just asking one condition. In such case, you use 'if ~ else if ~' sentence.

Let's take a look at an example of online shopping mall. Let's think of a case where you need to check if the name, phone number, e-mail, and address are correctly input to register as a member. If the name is not input correctly, tell the user to input the name again, if the phone number is not input correctly, tell the user to input the phone number again, and if the e-mail is not input correctly, tell the user to input the e-mail again, and the same for the address. 'if ~ else if ~' sentence is used in such a case where you are trying to process several conditions in a row.

Now, let's think of a case using repeated if sentences. It is the case where there is another if sentence in one if sentence.

It is the same as a sentence, 'If I were a bird and if I love you, I will fly to you'. First, you check if condition to see if I were a bird, and then check one more condition to see if I love you.

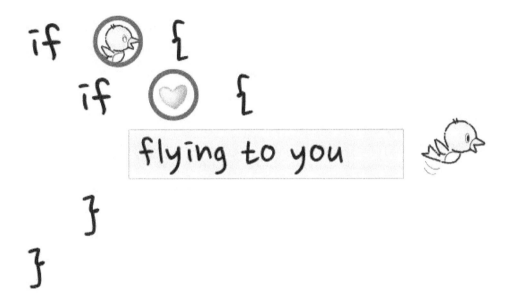

Next conditional sentence is Switch. Switch sentence also plays the role of processing commands according to the condition of if sentence. While If sentence compares one condition, Switch sentence compares several cases at once. If you use If~else if sentence, you can compare several conditions, but Switch sentence processes several cases corresponding to one condition.

```
switch (animal) {
    case 🐦:
        flying to you   🐦   break;

    case 🐷:
        walking to you   🐷   break;

    case 🐢:
        crawling to you   🐢   break;

    default:
        running to you   🚶   break;
}
```

To process for each case, you use case sentence, and if it does not correspond to any case, you process with default sentence. And you write the condition formula in Switch sentence.

Then, let's look at the example of 'If I were a bird, I could fly to you' which we used for learning If condition sentence. Check variable named ANIMAL which contains the types of animals, and if it is a bird, carry out the command 'flying to you', and if it is a pig, 'walking to you', and if it is a turtle, 'crawling to you'. If it is any other animal, let's think of carrying out the command 'running to you'.

Now, let's check the example of using Switch sentence with code. Use function called Date() to save the current date information into the variable called CURRENT_DATE. And then, use an internal function called getDate() to check the day of week information. Day of week information is a number starting from 0, which is Sunday. Through Switch sentence, check day of week information, and process the day of week information corresponding to each number through case sentence.

```
var d=new Date();

switch(d.getDay()) {
    case 0:
        document.write("Sunday");
        break;
    case 1:
        document.write ("Monday");
        break;
    case 2:
        document.write ("Tuesday");
        break;
    case 3:
        document.write ("Wednesday");
        break;
    case 4:
        document.write ("Thursday");
        break;
    case 5:
        document.write ("Friday");
```

```
            break;
        case 6:
            document.write ("Saturday");
            break;
        default:
            document.write ("I do not know");
            break;
    }
```

8. Loop Sentence

For sentence is useful to check the condition and to process repeated tasks. Usually, it is carried out with an initial value and condition, and the method of increasing.

Let's assume that we went to an amusement park and bought tickets for 10 rides. There are 10 sections on the coupon, and you will receive a seal in each section to increase the number of rides every time you ride. The ticket inspector will check the number of seals on the ticket and let you ride until there are seals in all 10 sections. And when there are seals in all 10 sections, you will not be use the ticket any more.

In such a case, you use 'For' sentence. Like the array, it is better to have the habit of using 0, not 1 as the beginning number. Then, let's check with the program code.

```
var count;

for( count = 0 ; count <= 10 ; count++) {

    ................

}
```

Let's think of a case using For sentence for more complex case. It is the multiple loop concept which has For sentence in a For sentence. During the repeated processing, another repeated processing is within. We call the For sentence outside as an outer loop and the For sentence inside as an inner loop.

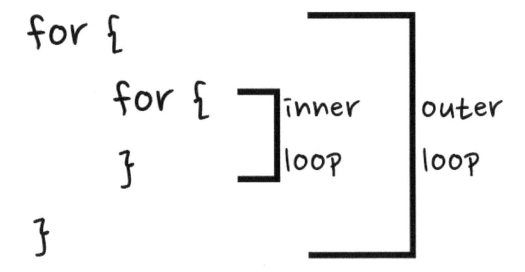

Is it a little difficult? Then, let's look at an easy and convenient example. You know the multiplication table. When we learn the multiplication table, you increase the first digit and then increase the second digit one by one, like 2 X 1=2, 2 X 2=4, ... The outer loop increases the first digit and the inner loop increases the second digit from 1 to 9, and perform the multiplication. Let's verify it with a program code.

```
var i;

var j;


for( i = 2 ; i <= 9 ; i++) {

    for( j = 1 ; j <= 9 ; j++) {

        .................

    }

}
```

Next loop sentence is While sentence. While sentence is very similar to For sentence, but it has a small difference. In terms of looking at the condition and processing repeated tasks, it is similar to For sentence, but it does not set the number of repetition and decides just by looking at the condition. That is, without increasing a counter as in For sentence, it makes the decision just by looking at the condition.

```
var count;


while ( count < 5 ) {

...............

count++

}
```

If you need to carry out the task at least once, you use do~while sentence. The above For or While sentence first checks the condition, so if the condition is not met, it may not carry out the task at all. On the other hand, in do~while sentence, it first carries out do sentence once and then compares the condition, and if the condition is met, it carries out the task again.

In which occasion do you use do~while sentence, which carries out the task at least once? There may be many examples, but let's think of a case of a user log-in in an online shopping mall. To log in as a registered user, you need to input the password. If you input the correct password on the first try, you will be able to log in without going through the loop, but if the password is incorrect, you need to repeat the password input. Do~while sentence is used in such case.

While sentence only checks the condition so if the condition is always met by mistake, it may fall into an endless loop, so you need to be careful. If you only check the condition and if the condition does not change, it continues the repetition and there may be a case where the program never stops.

You may force to stop the repetition in For sentence or While sentence. What will be the case? Let's say a patient with blood type A is in a critical condition and requires blood transfusion. Let's think of a case looking for a person with blood type A among the blood donators. If you find a person with blood type A during the search, you don't have to search the remaining persons' blood types. In such case, if you want to end the loop any time in a loop, you use the command Break. When the program encounters Break, it immediately exits the loop and processes the next command.

```
while
    ......
    if blood_type == 'A';
        break;
    ......
```

When you process repeating sentences such as For sentence and While sentence, there is a case skipping to the next turn without exiting the loop. As the above example, let's say that you are looking for a person with blood type A, but this time, there are many patients, and you are looking for all blood donators with blood type A, not just looking for one person. You look at the blood type, and if it is not A, you immediately go to the next person, and if it is A, you write the name in the list and then go to the next person. As such, the command to go to the next turn without processing the following commands is Continue.

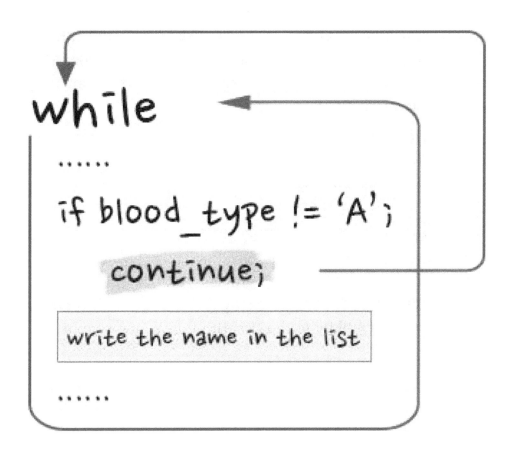

9. Event and Function

Event processing has different concept from the above methods. The above If, For, While, and Switch sentences process the condition according to the flow of the program. We call such method a Flow-driven development method. But as the program's user interface advances and as the interactions between user and program increase, a limitation was found in the existing simple flow processing method. If you need to process for an event such as, while a program is running, a user pressing a button or pressing keyboard, you need a new flow processing method. We call such even processing focused development type as Event-driven method.

Then, what are the events? Not just the actions of the user, such as clicking mouse, text input, and mouse cursor positioning on a button, but actions such as starting a screen or timer operation can be set as an event.

To understand the method of event operation, let's think of a space shuttle launch game. Let us all imagine the view of space shuttle launch. Count down progresses '10, 9, 8, 7, ,,,' and '1, 0, launch!' With the command, when you press the launch button, the space shuttle will fly to the sky with flames and roar.

What is the event here? Yes. Pressing(Clicking) a button is an event. The command to carry out when an event occurs is launching the space shuttle. We will name the function, which is the group of commands, to launch the space shuttle as space_Shuttle_Launch. Let's make the name of the button buttonFire. And let's look at the program code.

```
.........

<button id="buttonFire">Fire Suttle</button>

.........

<script>

function space_Shuttle_Launch()

{
```

```
······Please lanch a space shuttle·······..

}
var el = document.getElementById("buttonFire ");
el.addEventListener("click", space_Shuttle_Launch);
</script>
·········
```

Now, you will be able to roughly understand the event processing method. Then, let's think of event-driven method again through the 3 important concepts of the event processing.

The first concept is Event Target. It is the target to transfer the event when an event occurs. In our example, buttonFire becomes the event target.

The second important element is Event Listener. As the name says, it plays the role of listening the event. It listens to the contents about the flow and action of an event to see which command shall be called when an event occurs. In the program code, addActionListener is used, and when an action such as pressing mouse button occurs, event is created. When an event occurs, it carries out the command space_Shuttle_Launch().

The last important concept is Event Handler. It is the group of commands how to process the event when an event occurs. You can easily see that space_Shuttle_Launch() is the event handler. As in the above example, to process several commands, event handler is usually made as a form of a function, which is a group of commands.

Now it is time to focus on a new word 'function' in front of space_Shuttle_Launch().

What is a function? Function is one of the fundamental building blocks in languages. A function is a procedure, a set of statements that perform a task or calculate a value.

Can you understand? Don't too much worry even it is not clear to you. Let us think a very simple example. We want to make a calculator function to repeat calculation works. We will make a calculator function and send two values and operator like plus, minus, multiply and divide. Then our function will return a result value. That is function.

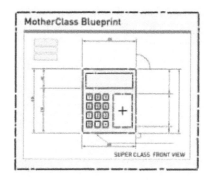

We have to define three items for each function. The first mandatory item is the name of the function. The second is a list of parameters to the function. In our previous calculator function, we have to send A, B values and operator. These are parameters and which are separated by commas. The last point we have to keep is to enclose curly brackets { ..} all statements in a function.

Let us make the calculator function now. We will define the function name as calculator. And list of three parameters valueA, valueB and operator. Of course we have to enclose all statements in the function with curly brackets as below.

```
.........

function calcluators(valueA, valueB, operator)

{

    var returnValue;

    .......

    If (operator == '*') {

      returnValue = valueA * valueB;

    }

     return returnValue;

}
.........
```

10. Class and Object

Have you heard about the concept of the object oriented programming? It is a little difficult to understand in the beginning. If you do not understand the concept from the beginning, you will complain keep complaining about the difficult and complex structure. Existing programming methods had to make all the actions used in sequential order. Simple programs have no problem, but if it is complex and there are many cases, it is difficult to make, and it is also difficult to apply the changes. But in the object oriented programming, the concept is that you make a good blueprint with the units of the parts called classes and make the actual unit function into an Object for free combination and reuse.

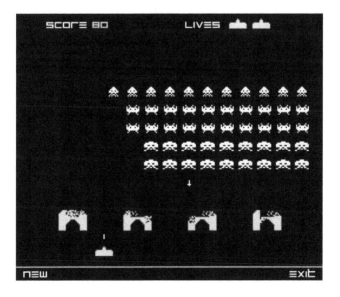

When I was young, there was a famous game called Invader. It is a game where group of spacecrafts invades earth from outer space, and our cannons shoot the cannonballs to defeat the enemy spacecrafts. It is a very simple game but it is a masterpiece equipped with the basics of a game.

In this game, many of the same forms such as enemy spacecrafts, cannons, and cannonballs are made and they move independently from each other. If we design the spacecraft, the cannon, and the cannonball as classes and make several objects by copying them, we can control each of them. If the user pushes fire button, then a new cannonball is fired, and among many spacecrafts, only the spacecraft hit by the cannonball will explode, and the rest will move independently. The created object can have individual data value or use the functions independently. As such, the method of efficiently operating a program centered on an object is called the object oriented programming.

In the object oriented programming, class is compared to a blueprint. Yes. You cannot actually use the class itself, but it is a structure that well organized the data values and the functions that the objects to be created in the future need to have.

In a class, the variables storing the data are called fields, and the functions to process are called methods. Class is a group combining fields and methods. Let's design the enemy spacecraft in Invader as class with the name of Spacecraft.

What are the data required to control the movements of the spacecrafts? First, you need x coordinate and y coordinate, and you need to designate the speed of the movement. So we will make number type xPosition and yPosition, and a field called speed.

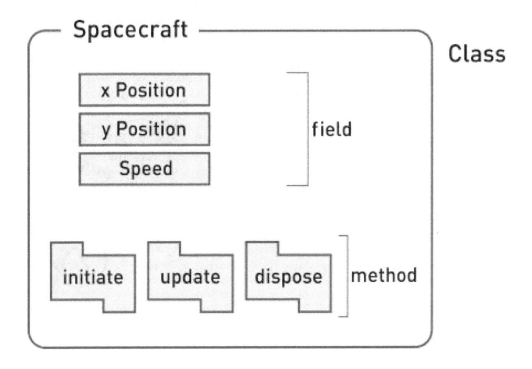

Then, what are the required methods? First, you need the initialization method to make spacecrafts, method to change the location and speed, and you can also think of a function to remove the spacecraft when it is hit by a cannonball. We will name the method to initialize the spacecrafts as initiate, name the function to change the location and speed as update, and design the method named dispose which removes the spacecraft.

As explained above, class is just an abstract blueprint, and to store actual data or to use the designed functions, you need to make objects. As such, we call the action of making objects with individual names based on the contents defined in the object as Instantiation. Then, with one class, how many objects can you make? There is no limitation of the number of the objects that can be made with one class. Therefore, it means that you can significantly improve the reusability of a program. You can assign a separate value to each created object.

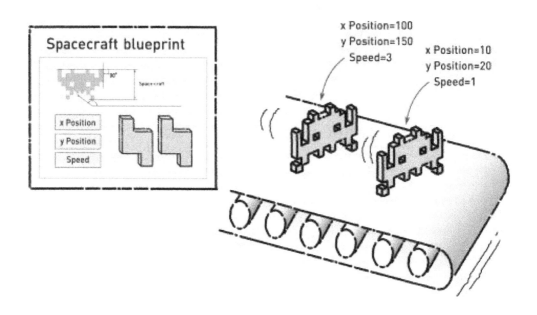

We understood the concept of the object oriented programming, class, and object. Then, shall we look at how to use the classes through the actual program code? Actually, JavaScript is not a language made based on a perfect object oriented programming, so it plays the role of the class using the functions. Strictly speaking, functions and classes are different concepts, but we will name them as classes instead of functions for the purpose of learning the objected oriented language.

```
var Spacecraft = {

    xPosition:100,

    yPosition:100,

    speed:100,

initiate:function(xPosition, yPosition, speed){

    ......

},

update:function(xPosition, yPosition, speed){
```

```
    ......
},
dispose:function(){

    ......

}
```

We will make Spacecraft class, which was stated above as an example, using JavaScript function. Among several methods to make class, we will organize them with the Object literal method that can express most closely to the object oriented programming.

As we have seen in the above example code, you can declare the class named Spacecraft as 'var Spacecraft...', but there are a few things to consider.

First, you declare a field, which is a variable to be used in the class. In the example, fields such as xPosition, yPosition, and speed are made, and the initial values are input. Then, you make methods, which are the internal functions named as initiate, update, and dispose.

```
var Spacecraft = {

    xPosition:100,

    yPosition:100,

    speed:100,

    initiate:function(xPosition, yPosition, speed){

        this.xPosition = xPosition;

        this.yPosition = yPosition;

        this.speed = speed;

        ......
```

```
    },

    update:function(xPosition, yPosition, speed){

        ......

    },

    dispose:function(){

        ......
```

The next concept to consider is Accessor. JavaScript does not provide a special key word for access control for the members and for information hiding. We will explain with the concept of general objected oriented language.

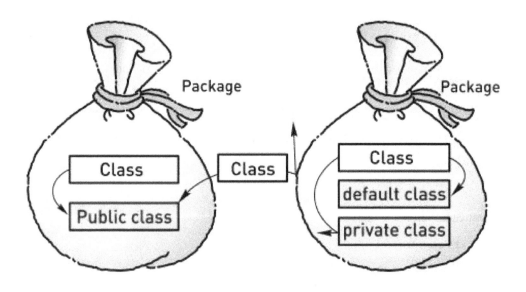

In the object oriented language, there are various forms of accessors to control the access to the classes, and we will look at the 3 representative accessors commonly used. If you access a class without any restriction from outside the package containing the common classes, you use an accessor called public. If there is no need to access from outside, and if you only allow access to the classes inside the package, you can safely access to the classes using the accessor called default, which has no accessor marking. And if you want to block the access to the class from outside regardless of the package, you use the accessor named private.

If you omit the accessor of a class in general object oriented language, it is basically recognized as default. But in JavaScript, without the concept of the accessor managing closed member by itself such public, default, or private, all methods and attributes are defined as public. Therefore, the developer needs to directly develop a private member in JavaScript. Then, shall we look at the codes for Spacecraft class including the fields and methods explained above?

We put all of the 3 fields and methods explained above into the class. In general object oriented language, to be able to directly access the field data value from outside, you use the accessor public, and if you only use it inside the class, you use the accessor private to block the external usage. In JavaScript, you cannot use the accessor private, so the developer shall consider all of xPosition, yPosition, and speed field as internal area variables that are not accessed from outside. To change the value of a field, you need to access through a method called initiate that can access from outside.

Now, you probably understood sufficiently about the concept of the classes and how to use them. This time, let's find out the process of the instantiation which makes Spacecraft class into a usable object. We will make an example using Spacecraft class which we made above in the class in the game Invader.

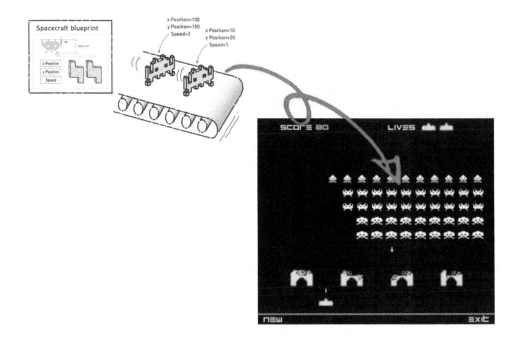

As we have seen above, we use Spacecraft class which we made above in the class called Invader. First, you make a field named instantSpacecraft to contain the object of the form of Spacecraft. And then, use operator new to create a new object from Spacecraft class. Then, assign adequate x, y coordinates and initial speed value to the internal function initiate inside the created object to initialize the variables. If you declare the variables to contain the objects as such and instantiate the corresponding classes with operator new, you can make as many objects as you wish.

```
var Invader = {

    instantSpacecraft:null,

    ............

    instantSpacecraft = new Spacecraft ();

    instantSpacecraft .initiate(startX,startY,invaderSpeed);
```

```
    ............
}
```

Then, let's find out how to use the methods inside the object after making the object.

To use the methods in the same class, you just need to call the corresponding method name. Let's think of a case that, in Spacecraft class, before removing a spacecraft, to mark the final location, you call update method. In such case, as in the following code, you just need to call update method in dispose method.

```
var Spacecraft = {

    xPosition:100,

    yPosition:100,

    speed:100,

    initiate:function(xPosition, yPosition, speed){

        ......

    },

    update:function(xPosition, yPosition, speed){

        ......

    },

    dispose:function(){

        this.update(xPosition, yPosition, speed);

    }

}
```

This time, let's think of a case that uses internal method inside another object created in a different class. There is a good example above. Let's think of a case calling update method to change the location of a certain Spacecraft object created in Invader class.

```
var Invader = {

    instantSpacecraft:null,

    ............

    instantSpacecraft = new Spacecraft ();

    ............

    instantSpacecraft.update(startX,startY,invaderSpeed);

}
```

We created a new Spacecraft object with operator new in the field named instantSpacecraft. To call the method of the created object, you write the corresponding method using period('.'). In the above example, it is written as the form of 'instantSpacecraft.update(startX,startY,invaderSpeed);'.

To get or change the value of a field used inside an object, what can you do? You use the same method again. Inside the same class, you just need to write the field name, and to call from a different class, you can use a period.

```
var Invader = {

    instantSpacecraft:null,

    ............

    instantSpacecraft = new Spacecraft ();

    ............
```

```
    instantSpacecraft.speed = 5;

}
```

To increase the speed of the newly made spacecraft object instantSpacecraft, it is changing the speed value to 5 using a period. Those of you who studied the previous contents well probably have already guessed, but the variables of the external functions shall not be used directly. In other object oriented programming, when you block the direct access from outside the class by setting the accessor of all the fields including speed as private when you design Spacecraft class, an error will occur, but in JavaScript, such management shall be done by the developer. It is because that, in JavaScript, all access conditions are set as public.

β

The Ten Commandments of Cocos2d-JS

There are several frameworks to produce a game. Among those, we will use a framework named Cocos2d-JS. Cocos2d-JS uses JavaScript, which we already learned, and it is based on JavaScript, which is growing to become the industry standard. Therefore, it can be used in most of the web browsers and devices that supports JavaScript. It is an attractive game framework that can be used in various platforms with just a single development.

Cocos2d-JS was originally based on a language called Python. It was started from a meeting of 50 Python developers in Los Cocos region, Argentina, to develop an open source game library. And then, as it was ported for iPhone in 2008, it became famous as an open source game software.

Afterwards, Team-x in China developed it as a game framework named Cocos2d-x, which is based on C++. The biggest advantage of Cocos2d-x is that with just a single development, it can be used in various platforms such as iPhone, Android, Windows, Black Berry, etc., and PC platforms such as Windows, Mac, and Linux. Cocos2d-JS is a framework supporting JavaScript based on the advantages of Cocos2d-x.

I hope you will be able to understand the games easily and be more familiar with the programming using Cocos2d-JS.

1. Getting Started

Now, we are ready to start our game projects. We selected Cocos2d-JS in order to develop cross-platform games. Cocos2d-JS is one of the popular open source 2D game framework. You can deploy android, iOS mobile apps and even web game by single programming. It is based on JavaScript language which you've learned. So, I can suggest that Cocos2d-JS will reduce your efforts to learn and build game programming.

The first step we have to do is setup Cocos2d-JS programming environment. We will use cocos console commends later. The cocos console is based on Python. So, we have to install Python. Cocos console is based on Python 2.X. You can downloand it from the Python official site at https://www.python.org. Actually, it is installed on MacOS by default.

As I mentioned, Cocos2d supports android, iOS and other platforms. If you want to develop iOS apps, it is better to use MacOS machine. We have to install some pre requirements like Android NDK(Native Development Kit) in order to develop android apps both Windows and MacOS.

Now we are ready to install Cocos2d framework. Actually Coco2d-JS is a part of Cocos2d-x bundle. So, you need to download a Cocos2d-x bundle from the official site at https://www.cocos2d-x.org. When you download Cocos2d-x file, extract zip file. You can extract any place. Let me place 'cocos2d-x' folder at 'C:\Dev\cocos2d-x' in Window OS and '/Users/⟨⟨my computer name⟩⟩/Dev/cocos2d-x' folder in MacOS.

Then open the terminal on MacOS or command prompt window on Windows OS. Move to the extracted folder and run the following command.

```
python setup.py
```

We will use 'Cocos Command-line tool' and a text editor. Cocos2d-JS is open source tools. There are pros and cons. Definitely it is good thing to use it freely. But, there is insufficient support to develop compare to other commercial IDE(Integrated Development Environment). But, don't too much worry. We can choose several good tools to develop. Let us use one of open-source editors 'Visual Studio Code' (https://code.visualstudio.com/)with Cocos Command-line tool. It support JavaScript coding-hint, integrated terminal and other functions. And it can be used Windows, MacOS and Linux as well.

Now let us take a look at major Cocos Command-line tools.

The first important command is to create a new project. You can refer a cocos project creation command as below.

```
cocos new <game name> -p <package identifier> -l <language> -d <location>
```

If you want to create a new project name 'brickBreaker' and package name 'com.creapple.brickbreaker', we will make the Cocos2d-JS project at the same place like this command.

```
cocos new brickBreaker -p com.creapple.brickbreaker -l js
```

Once you've create the project, it is time to refer a file structure of a Cocos2d-JS project. Cocos2d-JS engine generates bundles of folders and files by 'cocos new~' command.

It generate three major folders. The first folder 'frameworks' contains actual Cocos2d-JS engine and related files for native deployment, JSB(JavaScript Binding) and others. The next folder's name is 'res'. It contains all images, sound files and other resources that are referred in the game. The remain folder is 'src' folder which contains all JavaScript files for our game.

Now let us take a look at major files which was created in a project. We'd like to focus on 'main.js' and 'project.json' files. When you open 'main.js' file, you can assume it is the entry point of the Cocos2d-JS project. The project will be started by executing 'onStart' function in this file. There are some configuration commands in the file like setting the resolution size by 'cc.view.setDesignResolutionSize' function.

```
cc.game.onStart = function(){
    var sys = cc.sys;

    ......

    // Setup the resolution policy and design resolution size
    cc.view.setDesignResolutionSize(320, 560, cc.ResolutionPolicy.SHOW_ALL);

    ......

};
```

The next file 'project.json' has meta information about the Cocos2d-JS project. It contains serveral project information like project type, debugMode, frame rate and so on. There are modules and related JavaScript files definition as well.

```
{
    "project_type": "javascript",
    "debugMode" : 1,
    "showFPS" : false,
    "frameRate" : 60,
    "noCache" : false,
    "id" : "gameCanvas",
    "renderMode" : 0,
    "engineDir":"frameworks/cocos2d-html5",

    "modules" : ["cocos2d"],
    "jsList" : [
        "src/config/Resource.js",
        "src/config/GameConfig.js",
```

```
.......

    ]

}
```

When you create a blank Brick Breaker project, you can copy files or codes from completed sample code files. You can get it from creApple web site http://www.creapple.com.

Now let us back to Cocos commands. The next command we have to learn is about compile a project. It is necessary to compile a project in order you make change to your code. The command is formatted as below.

```
cocos compile <path to your project> -p <platform> -m <mode> -o <output
directory>
```

I will explain some options on it. -p is the platform you are compiling for. -m is mode, debug or release with the default being debug if this parameter is not specified. If we are already in current location and want to make iOS app, then we can make it short like this.

```
cocos compile . -p ios -m release
```

Once we have created a project we can run it from the running command-line. It is the run cocos command.

```
cocos run -s <path to your project> -p <platform>
```

We can simplify a command when we run web project at the same place as formatted. We can also specify to run in debug or release mode using the optional -m parameter. Excluding this parameter defaults to debug. When you run a web project, you can easily check working and features of the project in a web browser.

```
cocos run . -p web -m release
```

Once you are ready to deploy your project, you can use cocos deploy command for deploying it. The command is as below.

```
cocos deploy -s <path to your project> -p <platform> -m <mode>
```

It is a quite useful command to deploy web project. We can simply deploy web files and place it to web server like apache Tomcat and so on. Actually, I prefer to use web deploy command in order to check project code working. When you run it, you can copy web deploy files from '/publish/html5' folder.

```
cocos deploy . -p web -m release
```

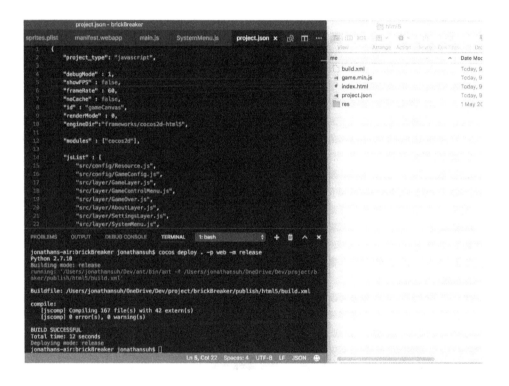

2. Structure of a Framework

Let's study the structure of Cocos2d framework which we use for game production. Cocos2d framework is made of the layer structure of several important classes.

The highest level class is Node. Node class has various attributes such as location, color, transparency, size, etc. It can also use scheduler to express movement. The child classes that inherit Node class according to the characteristics of object oriented programming can use various properties of Node class.

The representative classes used in Cocos2d framework are Director, Scene, Layer, and Sprite. But the names of the game production classes are similar to the terms used in movies. Then, let's think of the movie scenes familiar to us for easy understanding of the game class concept.

Let's think of the last duel scene of an action movie that we frequently watch. Usually, the main character, who is the apostle of justice overcomes the difficulties and makes the final duel with the head of the villain. In the final duel, the main character tries his best in the duel, and when he wins, the movie comes to a happy ending.

Then, shall we list up the elements composing the final duel in the movie as Director, Scene, Layer, and Sprite class concept?

All scenes of a movie from the beginning to the end are usually directed by one director. In the games, like the director in a movie, there is also a Director class that oversees how to compose the scenes and flow of the game.

One movie is composed of many scenes, and usually the films are shot scene by scene. The scene of the final duel is also one of many scene units composing the movie. Also in a game, there is a Scene class to manage the flow of the game in the units of scenes.

One Scene may be composed of one Layer, or sometimes composed by combining several Layers. The duel scene of the two main characters seems to be overlapping 'Duel Layer' and 'Background Layer'. In Cocos2d framework, there is Layer class that manages Layer.

The characters (Sprites) appearing in the duel scene will be the main character and the head of the villain. The specific class displayed on the screen such as static image or animation in the game is Sprite.

Director	Scene	Layer	Sprite

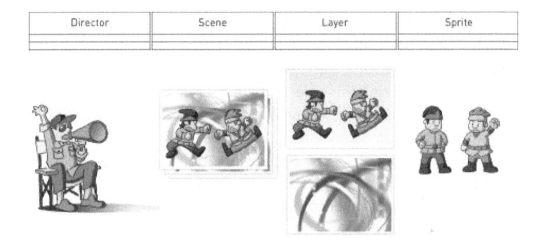

As such, with the same method of listing up the scenes in a movie as class concept, let's arrange Garden Keeper game with Director, Scene, Layer and Sprite class concept.

Director	Scene	Layer	Sprite

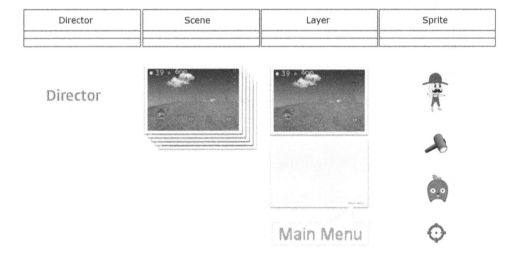

As there is a director in a movie, also in Cocos2d-JS framework, there is a class called 'Director'. Director is a Singleton class that only one exists in one game application, and it creates and manages main view which the user actually sees, and plays the role of controlling when to move to the next Scene.

Then, we will explain by looking at the source code in the game. When we studied the structure of a game, we explained the role of Loader that starts the game. In Garden Keeper game, the program playing this role is 'main.js'. Here, we use director class that composes the screen of the game and manages the flow. First, make a Scene class named 'SystemMenu.js' which will be used as the initial screen of the game and instance by 'scene()' method. Then, director instance runs the initial menu screen of the game, SystemMenuScene instance using a command called 'runScene'.

(/src/main.js)

```
cc.game.onStart = function(){

    ........

    cc.view.adjustViewPort(true);

    cc.view.setDesignResolutionSize(480, 320, cc.ResolutionPolicy.SHOW_ALL);
    cc.view.resizeWithBrowserSize(true);

    //load resources

    cc.LoaderScene.preload(g_resources, function () {

        cc.director.runScene(new SystemMenuScene());

    }, this);

};

cc.game.run();

    .........
```

As we list up the game structures, we composed the game screens with 'Main Menu', 'Game Play', 'Option', 'About' and 'Game Over'. Therefore, we shall compose the game with five Scenes. In the above initial screen that we moved to, if you press 'Option' button, the screen changes to a Scene changing the settings of the game. If you look at the program code, first you make a Scene class instance with the name 'scene', and then replace it with a new Scene using a command called runScene of a director class.

(/src/layer/SystemMenu.js)
....

```
onSettings:function (pSender) {
    this.onButtonEffect();
    var scene = new cc.Scene();
    scene.addChild(new SettingsLayer());
    cc.director.runScene(new cc.TransitionFade(1.2, scene));
},
```
....

The next class is Layer class. One or more Layers can be attached to a Scene. If you see the above program code carefully, you can see that only one Layer named 'SettingsLayer' is used in the Scene that can change the settings of the game. But in the Scene displaying a new game, there are two Layers. First, there is a Layer named 'GameLayer.js' that runs the game. And there is also a transparent layer named 'GameControlMenu.js' that has a button at the bottom right to return to the main screen. Layer is like a transparent drawing paper, and you can show several layers in overlap like here.

(/src/layer/SystemMenu.js)
....

```
onNewGame:function (pSender) {
    GM.LEVEL = 0;
    GM.SCORE = 0;
```

```
//load resources
cc.Loader.preload(g_maingame, function ()
    cc.audioEngine.stopMusic();
    cc.audioEngine.stopAllEffects();
    var scene = new cc.Scene();
    scene.addChild(new GameLayer());
    scene.addChild(new GameControlMenu());
    cc.director.runScene(new cc.TransitionFade(1.2, scene));
}, this);
},
.........
```

The last class is Sprite. In GameLayer that runs the game, all of the various Sprites in the game such as Hammer, Keeper, Mole, and Target appear. Then, let's take a look at the program code to make timer Sprite that indicates the remaining time in GameLayer game screen. There are several methods to make Sprite class, and to use timer figure 'Timmer.png' as a Sprite, you use method called 'cc.Sprite'. You make a Sprite instance as such and put it in the variable named 'timmerLogo', and include in GameLayer using addChild command.

(/src/layer/GameLayer.js)

```
.........

var timmerLogo = new cc.Sprite("#Timmer.png");

.........

this.addChild(timmerLogo, 1, 5);
this.lbTimmer = new cc.LabelBMFont(this._time, res.s_scorefont_fnt, 40);
this.lbTimmer.x = 70;
```

```
this.lbTimmer.y = winSize.height - 30;
this.addChild(this.lbTimmer, 1000);
.........
```

In addition to director, Scene, Layer and Sprite class, there is also Label class that indicates score or name. If you look below the code making timer Sprite, you can see the contents of making Label named 'lbTimmer' which indicates the time.

For an example of Menu class, let's check with a menu returning to the initial screen, which is in 'GameControlMenu.js'. In one menu, there may be several menu items. Here, we will make a menu item named 'systemMenu' and will attach to Menu class named 'menu'.

(/src/layer/GameControlMenu.js)

```
var systemMenu = new cc.MenuItemFont("Main Menu", this.onSysMenu);
var menu = new cc.Menu(systemMenu);
.........
```

3. Actions

We studied about Node class used in Cocos2d framework and director, Scene, Layer and Sprite class which inherited the Node class. Common attributes and functions of the classes are developed in the Node, which is the super class, and the attributes and functions required for the purpose are developed in director, Scene, Layer and Sprite class, which are sub classes.

As they keep inheriting, in each class, the objectives and functions are already developed, and it is so convenient that we need to make only the necessary parts according to the set method. It is the advantage of the object oriented program that we learned.

This time, we will also study one more useful class that inherits the Node class. It is the Action class that develops a function that can move classes in various motions such as move, rotate, and jump, etc. Action class has various attributes such as position, rotation, scale, etc. to express the movements.

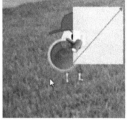

Then, let's understand Action class by looking at Garden Keeper game example. When you touch the gardener, a red dot appears, and if you pull it while pressing it and let it go, the red dot moves back to the original location. It does not just move, but it also moves fast and then approaches the original point slowly.

Then, we will explain by looking at the example program code. The command displaying the movement of the red dot is moveBy. As we see the contents of the example, it is a command to move in x axis for 1 sec. by the value of this._deltaXvalue variable, and in y axis by the value of this._deltaYvalue variable.

(/src/layer/GameLayer.js)

```
releaseHammer:function( event ) {

    if( this._state == STATE_PLAYING ) {

        var hammer = Hammer.createHammer(this._deltaXvalue,this._deltaYvalue);

        this.addChild(hammer);

        var move = cc.moveBy(1, cc.p(this._deltaXvalue,this._deltaYvalue));

        var move_ease = move.clone().easing(cc.easeExponentialOut());

        var fade_out = cc.fadeOut(1.0);

        var seq = cc.sequence(move_ease, fade_out);

        this._point.runAction(seq);

        this._arrowBox.runAction(cc.fadeOut(2.0));

        if(GM.EASYMODE) {

            this._target.runAction(cc.fadeOut(2.0));

        }
```

The command to have change in the movement such as first move fast and then move slow is ease. Ease has various forms, and among them, we use a command called easeExponentialOut that has rapid decrease of the change as time goes. And you can also see an Actions command called fadeOut which changes the transparency for 1 sec. to make it transparent.

To run Actions, you use a command named runAction. You may run one Actions, but you may also want to run several commands in sequence. Command to use in such case is Sequence. In the example code, it runs two commands Move and Fade in sequence.

There is also Actions called jumpBy that makes an object jump. The first value '1' of jumpBy command in the example means to move for 1 sec. The second variable represents the location of the object. The third '10' indicates the height of the jump and the last '2' means the number of jumps.

(/src/sprite/Mole.js)

```
jumpMole:function () {
    var actionUp = cc.jumpBy (1, cc.p(0, 0), 10, 2);
    var delay = cc.delayTime (0.25);
    this.runAction(
        cc.sequence (actionUp, delay));
},
```

Next, let's look at Actions called rotateBy which makes an object rotate. The first value '1.0' of rotateBy command in the example means to move for 1 sec., and the second value '360' is the angle of movement in that time. Another words, it means rotating one round in 1 second. If you use 'repeatForever' command here, the object will keep rotating. If you use this Actions, you can make the flying Hammer keep rotating.

(/src/sprite/Hammer.js)

```
......

var rotate = cc.rotateBy(1.0, 360);

var repeat = rotate.repeatForever();

this.runAction(repeat);

......
```

There is also Actions called scaleTo which changes the size of the object. In Brick Breaker, which is the first game, if you keep missing the ball, life is decreased, the size of the big bar decreases, and a new bar is created. You make Sprite named 'batSprite', and first enlarge the size to 8 times, and then reduce the size of the bar using scaleTo. The first value '0.5' is, as you guessed, the time for the change. The second represents the size of x axis in the meantime, and the third represents the size of y axis. The two values are all '1', so it means to return to the original size.

(/src/sprite/Bat.js)

```
this.batSprite = new cc.Sprite(res.s_bat2);

......

this.batSprite.scale = 8;

this.batSprite.runAction(cc.scaleTo(0.5, 1, 1));

......
```

4. Coordinate System

In a screen, to designate the location of the object, you need to understand the concepts of coordinate system and anchor of Cocos2d. Coordinate and anchor become the standards to show and move the object in the screen.

Who made the coordinate system? Yes. As you learned in interesting Mathematics and Physics, the coordinate system is a method made by the great Mathematician Descartes to efficiently express the location. So we call the coordinate system as the coordinate system of Descartes.

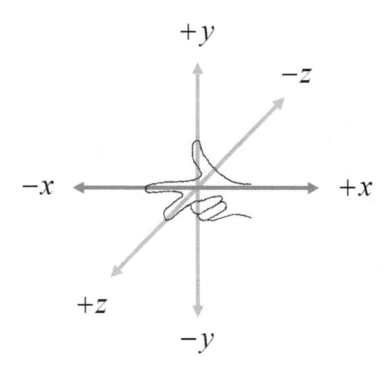

The coordinate system can be divided to the two systems according to *z* axis direction, right hand coordinate system and left hand coordinate system. In Cocos2d framework that we use, we use the right hand coordinate system as in the following figure.

First, let me explain *x* and *y* axis coordinate concept. Let's think of the *x* and *y* axis coordinates of the three objects, the gardener in Garden Keeper game, timer representing the time, and mole representing the score, using the locations of the objects. We will express the locations of the three objects in the coordinate system as in the following figure. Timer is above the gardener, and mole is displayed on its right side.

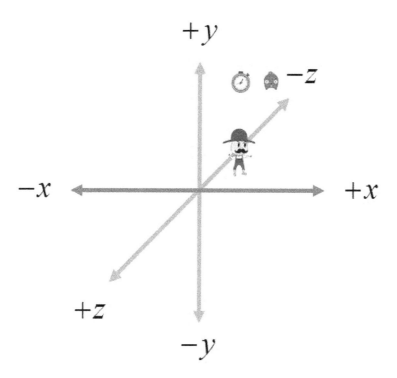

Then, let's look at the coordinates in the program code for better understanding. The variable representing the gardener is 'this._keeper', timer is 'timmerLogo', and mole display is 'scoreLogo'. And if you look at the code of '/config/GameConfig.js' which gathered the setting values, the values for GAME.KEEPER.XPOSITION, GAME.KEEPER.YPOSITION and g_hideMolePos constant are defined. Since the width of the game screen is 480 and height is 320, so the value of winSize.height is 320. As a result, when you sum it all up, gardener's x and y xcoordinate is (80, 80), timer's is (30, 290), and mole display's is (120, 290).

(/src/config/GameConfig.js)

```
......

GAME.KEEPER = {

          XPOSITION:80,

          YPOSITION:80

};

var g_hideMolePos = cc.p( 120, 290 );
```

(/src/layer/GameLayer.js)

```
......

timmerLogo.attr({

     scale: 0.5,

     x: 30,

     y: winSize.height - 30

});

scoreLogo.attr({

     scale: 0.5,
```

```
    x: g_hideMolePos.x,

    y: g_hideMolePos.y

});

......

this._keeper.x = GAME.KEEPER.XPOSITION;

this._keeper.y = GAME.KEEPER.YPOSITION;
```

This time, let's study the concept of z coordinate. If you disassemble the screen of Garden Keeper game in z axis direction, it can be classified to gardener, grass, bird, and sky as in the figure.

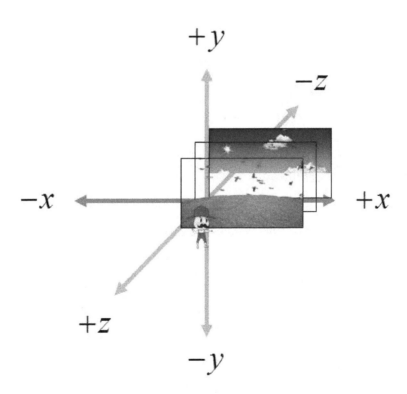

In Cocos2d, the location of z coordinate is managed by the concept of z-order. The default value of z-order is 0, and if the number is less than 0, the object is located behind, and if it bigger than 0, the object is located in front. The value of z-order is defined by the second value when you addChild the object. When you look at the program code, z-order value is not separately designated for 'this._keeper', which means the gardener, but the default value is '0' and z-order for 'this._backGlass', which means the grass, is designated as '-5', so it is located behind the gardener. The z-order of 'this._backTileMap', which is the drawing of the flying bird, is '-7', and z-order of 'this._backSky', which represents the sky, is '-10'. Now can you understand the location in z axis direction?

(/src/layer/GameLayer.js)

```
......

this._keeper = new Keeper();

this._keeper.x = GAME.KEEPER.XPOSITION;

this._keeper.y = GAME.KEEPER.YPOSITION;

this.addChild(this._keeper);

......

this._backGlass = new cc.Sprite("#glassBg.png");

......

this.addChild(this._backGlass, -5);

this._backTileMap = new cc.TMXTiledMap(res.s_backGround);

this.addChild(this._backTileMap, -7);

......

this._backSky = new cc.Sprite("#skyBg.png");

......

this.addChild(this._backSky, -10);
```

So far, we studied the concept of the coordinate system. This time, we will study how to adjust the location of an object through the concept of anchor. Anchor point means the location standard of Sprites, Menus, or Label, etc. included in the screen. Anchor point has the range from (0, 0) to (1.0, 1.0). Then, let's check the location according to the anchor point by looking at the figure. For example, if anchor point is (0.5, 0.5), the center of the object is located at *x* and *y* coordinate. Please check the locations of the remaining anchor points through the example.

(/src/main.js)
```
var AnchorPointCenter = new cc.Point(0.5, 0.5);

var AnchorPointBottomLeft = new cc.Point(0, 0);

var AnchorPointBottomRight = new cc.Point(1, 0);

var AnchorPointTopRight = new cc.Point(1, 1);

var AnchorPointTopLeft = new cc.Point(0, 1);

var AnchorPointTop = new cc.Point(0.5, 1);
```

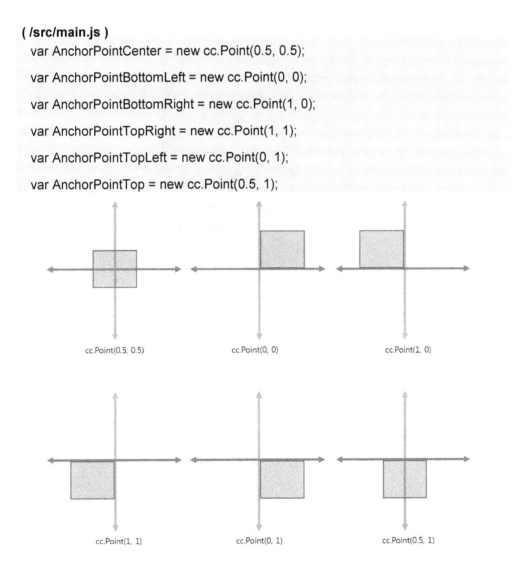

cc.Point(0.5, 0.5)   cc.Point(0, 0)   cc.Point(1, 0)

cc.Point(1, 1)   cc.Point(0, 1)   cc.Point(0.5, 1)

5. Events

As we learn about the programming, we learned the concept of an event. I understand that you all sufficiently know about the event, but don't worry even if you don't know its contents well. If you look at the examples of the events in the game, you will sufficiently understand the concept and usage of the event.

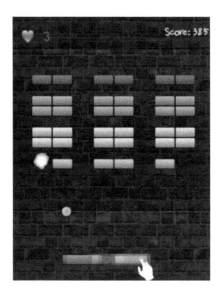

Let's take a look at the example of Block Breaking game that we made. You can move the bar which hits the moving ball using mouse, touch, or keyboard. Let's think of an example using mouse. If you press the bar with mouse and move to the right, the bar moves to the right, and if you move the mouse to the left, it will also move to the left. In smart phones, you can make the same motion by touching with finger instead of mouse. In PC, you can move the bar by pressing the arrow button in the keyboard.

As such, a motion of the user using mouse, touch or keyboard is called an event. Pressing the mouse is an event, pressing the keyboard is an event, and touching the screen is also an event. In devices like smart phones, if there is an acceleration sensor, tilting the device can also be used as an event.

Then, let me explain by looking at the program code. First, to use mouse, keyboard, touch or acceleration sensor, you need to declare to use them as in the following code. We will use keyboard, mouse and touch event in Block Breaking game.

(/src/layer/GameLayer.js)

```
if (cc.sys.capabilities.hasOwnProperty('keyboard')) {

    cc.eventManager.addListener({

        event: cc.EventListener.KEYBOARD,

    ......

if (cc.sys.capabilities.hasOwnProperty('mouse')) {

    cc.eventManager.addListener({

        event: cc.EventListener.MOUSE,

    ......

if (cc.sys.capabilities.hasOwnProperty('touches')) {

    cc.eventManager.addListener({

        prevTouchId: -1,

        event: cc.EventListener.TOUCH_ALL_AT_ONCE,
```

You declared to use the event, and now let's look at the part handling the mouse and touch events. In Block Breaking game, mouse and touch events are different, but they perform the common task. It receives the motion of an event and moves the bar accordingly. The common task is defined in 'processEvent' function. Among several touch events, we use 'onTouchesMoved', which is generated when bar is touched and moved. Event shall occur when mouse is moved, so 'onMouseMoved'event is used. In the two functions 'onTouchesMoved' and 'onMouseMoved' that receive the event, it sends the event to 'processEvent' function when the event occurs.

(/src/layer/GameLayer.js)

```
......

if (cc.sys.capabilities.hasOwnProperty('mouse')) {

    ......

    onMouseMove: function(event){
        if(event.getButton() == cc.EventMouse.BUTTON_LEFT)
            event.getCurrentTarget().processEvent(event);

......

if (cc.sys.capabilities.hasOwnProperty('touches')) {

    ......

    onTouchesMoved:function (touches, event) {
        if (this.prevTouchId != touch.getID())
            this.prevTouchId = touch.getId();
        else event.getCurrentTarget().processEvent(touches[0]);

......

processEvent:function( event ) {
    if( this._state == STATE_PLAYING ) {
```

```
var delta = event.getDelta();

var curPos = cc.p(this._bat.x, this._bat.y);

curPos= cc.pAdd( curPos, delta );

curPos = cc.pClamp(curPos, cc.p(0, 0),

                    cc.p(winSize.width, winSize.height) );

this._bat.x = curPos.x;

this._bat.y = this._batYPosition;

curPos = null;

},

......
```

Let's take a look at 'ProcessEvent'function, which lists up the commands to carry out when a mouse or touch event occurs. First, start after checking if the game is in play. If the game is in play, use 'getDelta' to check the size of the movement through the event. And then, set the location after the event occurrence by adding the changed size to the original location. Finally, match the location of the bar object with the name of 'this._bat' to the changed location. If you slowly go through the code according to the above explanation, you will easily understand.

This time, we will check the event handling using a keyboard. The event we are using is 'onKeyPressed'event, which is activated when a keyboard is pressed. It changes the array value corresponding to the key to true when a keyboard is pressed. We will make keyboard event become activated only when web browser is used. (…!cc.sys.isNative …) We will make the bar move to the corresponding direction when you press right or left arrow. And we will also make shortcut key. If you press 'a' on the keyboard, we will make the bar move to the left, and if you press 'd', we will make the bar move to the right. Of course, the bar can only move within the game screen range.

Please look at the following code which developed the defined contents into a program. When the user released the key, we will return the array value of the corresponding key to 'false' using the new keyboard event 'onKeyReleased'.

(/src/layer/GameLayer.js)

```
......

if (cc.sys.capabilities.hasOwnProperty('keyboard'))

    cc.eventManager.addListener({

            event: cc.EventListener.KEYBOARD,

            onKeyPressed:function (key, event) {

                GAME.KEYS[key] = true;

            },

            onKeyReleased:function (key, event) {

                GAME.KEYS[key] = false;

            }

    }, this);

......
```

(/src/sprite/Bat.js)

```
update:function (dt) {

    // Keys are only enabled on the browser

    if (!cc.sys.isNative) {

        if ((GAME.KEYS[cc.KEY.a] || GAME.KEYS[cc.KEY.left]) && this.x >= 0) {

            this.x -= dt * this.speed;

        }
```

```
if ((GAME.KEYS[cc.KEY.d] || GAME.KEYS[cc.KEY.right]) &&
    this.x <= winSize.width) {
    this.x += dt * this.speed;
    }
  }
},
......
```

Isn't it easy to understand the concept since you look at the event trough the actual examples in Block Breaking game? And, you probably thought that it was easy to understand intuitively even if you saw the program code for the first time. That is because that many methods are already developed in the upper classes, Node, Sprite, Layer class, etc., and we inherit and use them. We feel the efficiency of the object oriented program and the framework once again. The event we learned in this chapter is an important concept connecting the game program and the actions of the user. If you carefully take a look at the two example games and increase your skill, you will be able to easily handle any form of events.

6. Scheduler

We learned how to handle user commands using events in the game. A game usually carries out a new command using an event when the user inputs command with mouse, touch, or keyboard. But sometimes, you can make it carry out the command at every set time even if user did not make any input. In Cocos2d framework, scheduler functions to carry out the command at every set time.

Then, let's understand the concept of scheduler through the examples of usages in a game.

In Garden Keeper game, there is a timer function measuring time, and you need to decrease the number by one at every second. If the gardener throws the hammer, hammer performs a parabolic motion by keep changing *x* and *y* coordinate. At this time, the repetitive action of keep changing *x* and *y* coordinate is also performed by the scheduler. If the moles keep appearing and if the gardener throws the hammer, someone needs to keep watching to see if the hammer collided with a mole, and if there is a collision, mole shall be removed and score shall be increased. As such, the scheduler also performs the role of continuously watching the moles and the hammers.

There are two types of schedulers. There is 'Update selector' that acts at every frame even if time is not set, and there is 'Custom selector' that the user can set the time for action. Update Selector is recommended because it is faster and use less memory than Custom selector, but if certain time interval is required, you need to use Custom Selector.

Then, let's verify each one by looking at the program code. We will take a look at the contents related to the timer which measures the time of Garden Keeper game.

(/src/layer/GameLayer.js)

```
......

this.scheduleUpdate();

this.schedule(this.checkStageClear, 1);

......

checkStageClear:function () {
    if (this._state == STATE_PLAYING &&
        this._time) {
        this._time--;
```

```
        this.lbTimmer.setString(this._time);

        ......

   },
```

Timer function is activated every 1 second, so it uses Custom selector 'this.schedule(this.checkStageClear, 1)'. In the scheduler function, the first element 'this.checkStageClear' is the function name to call, and the second parameter '1' means to perform at every 1 second. Let's look at the contents of 'checkStageClear', which is the function run by the scheduler. When the value of 'this._time', variable meaning the game time, is not 0, it decreases the value by 1 and displays the changed time.

This time, we will look at 'scheduleUpdate', which is an update selector that is activated at every frame even if you don't set the time. If you look at the following program code, you can see that scheduler runs 'update' function at every frame. In the update function run by the scheduler, there is 'updateUI'function which shows the score of the screen and 'checkMoleCollide' function to check whether the moles and hammers collide. In the second function, every time the frame is changed, it checks whether the moles and hammers collide. You will learn the code to check the collision later, so you only need to understand the concept of the scheduler now.

(/src/layer/GameLayer.js)

```
   ......

   this.scheduleUpdate();
   this.schedule(this.checkStageClear, 1);

   ......

   update:function (dt) {
```

```
    if( this._state == STATE_PLAYING ) {

        this.updateUI();

        this.checkMoleCollide();

    }

},

......
```

Let me show you another example for better understanding. We will look at the concept of the scheduler through the parabolic motion of the hammer thrown by the gardener. In Constructor function 'ctor', which is run when Hammer class is created as an object, there is a scheduler 'scheduleUpdate' that is activated at every frame. Therefore, you can have the parabolic motion by changing x and y coordinate at every frame from the moment Hammer object is created. You will learn how to get x and y coordinate values using the principles of Mathematics and Physics later. Now, you only need to understand that the hammer performs parabolic motion using the scheduler until it gets near the ground.

(/src/sprite/Hammer.js)

```
......

ctor:function (xVelocity, yVelocity) {

    ......

    this.scheduleUpdate();

},

......

update:function (dt) {

    this._time = this._time + this._animationInterval;

    var xp = GAME.KEEPER.XPOSITION +  this._xVelocity * this._time;
```

```
var yp = GAME.KEEPER.YPOSITION +  this._yVelocity * this._time –
        0.5*this._gravity*Math.pow(this._time,2)


yp > (GAME.KEEPER.YPOSITION - 10)? this.setPosition(xp, yp) :
                                   this.destroy();
},
......
```

7. Animations

One of the important functions composing a game is the animation which you will learn now. Interesting game moves the main character and enemies in various forms to increase the effect and reality of the game. Originally, the term animation is from a Latin 'anima' meaning 'alive', and it means the movie technique repetitively filming several screens. In a game, animation means the function to show the screen continuously according to the time change by the result of the function or set method.

Then, let's understand the concept of animation through the actual example in Brick Breaker game. As a ball moves and hits a block, the block disappears. To increase the effect of the game, when a ball collides with a block, an explosion animation will be displayed along with the explosion sound effect.

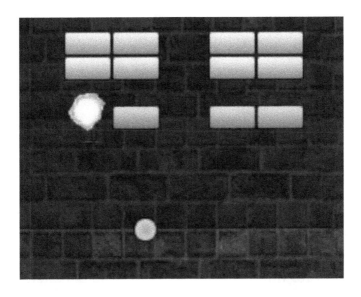

The basic principle of the animation in a game or a movie is sequentially showing several figures with different shape. Explosion animation also uses the same principle. You can make several figures from the start of an explosion to the end and show them sequentially. Then, first you need several figures, and second, you need program command to show the figures sequentially.

Then, let's prepare stepwise figures of the explosion, which are the first elements. As in the following figure, total of 40 figures are prepared by each step of the explosion screen. If you move the prepared 40 figures fast one by one, it looks like an actual explosion.

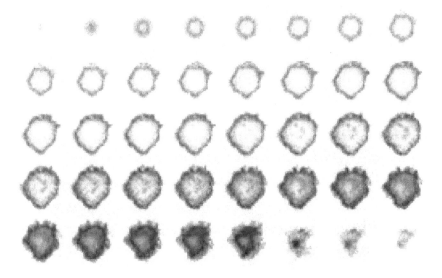

You can prepare and use each figure in separate files. But, we will make the animation by a little different method. For easy explanation, it is a method of positioning several figures sequentially in a file and saving the location information of each figure as separate information. Such method is called 'Sprite

Sheet Animation' as a specialized term, and the file containing the locations of the figures and the name information has 'plist'extension.

If you use such method, no matter how many figures are used in an animation, you can use only one figure file. It reduces the number readings of the files and also reduces the usage of memory, so it is widely used for animation.

One figure file made by gathering several figures to make an explosion animation is '/res/explosion.png'. Several figures are gathered in one file, so you need to manage the location of each figure and the information about the name. We manage the location of each figure and name information used in the explosion animation in XML format file 'explosion.plist'.

When you look at the contents of the file, information of each figure is defined in 'frames' key tag. The name of the first file is 'explosion_01.png', and its location is, as defined in 'frame' tag, between x and y coordinate (0, 0) and (32, 32). And the file size is, as in 'sourceSize' tag, 32 pixels in x and y axis. In such method, the remaining 39 figure file information is also defined.

The figure file information is defined in 'metadata' key tag. File name 'explosion.png' is in 'realTextureFileName' tag, file size is 512 pixels in x and y axis, and it is defined in 'size' tag.

(/res/explosion.plist)

```xml
<?xml version="1.0" encoding="UTF-8"?>

......

    <key>frames</key>
    <dict>
        <key>explosion_01.png</key>
        <dict>
```

```
        <key>frame</key>

        <string>{{0,0},{32,32}}</string>

            ......

        <key>sourceSize</key>

        <string>{32,32}</string>

        ......

    <key>metadata</key>

    <dict>

        ......

      <key>realTextureFileName</key>

      <string>explosion.png</string>

      <key>size</key>

      <string>{512,512}</string>

          ......

      </dict>

    </dict>

  </plist>
```

So far, we prepared figure file and plist file for the animation. Now, let's start to look at the code used in the program. As we decide the program structure, we decided to gather the contents related to the settings under 'src/config' folder. Information of the resources such as figure file or plist file are gathered in 'Resource.js' file which is under 'src/config'.

(/src/config/Resource.js)

```
var res = {

    ........

    s_explosion : 'res/explosion.png',

    ........

    s_explosion_plist : 'res/explosion.plist',

    ........
```

Figure file and plist file are registered as global variables, so we will use them in the game. In Cocos2d framework, you can register plist file in s_explosion_plist variable, and you can check the method of registering figure file in s_explosion variable in the following program code. And by making Explosion class into object, you create the animation using a method named 'sharedExplosion'.

(/src/layer/GameLayer.js)

```
......

cc.spriteFrameCache.addSpriteFrames(res.s_explosion_plist);

var explosionTexture = cc.textureCache.addImage(res.s_explosion);

this._explosions = new cc.SpriteBatchNode(explosionTexture);

this._explosions.setBlendFunc(cc.SRC_ALPHA, cc.ONE);

this.addChild(this._explosions);

Explosion.sharedExplosion();

......
```

This time, if you look at sharedExplosion function defined in Explosion class, you can see how to make an animation. Put 40 figures defined in figure file and plist file into an array named 'animFrames' suing for Loop. And 'cc.Animation.create(animFrames, 0.04)' code is the contents of making the animation with 0.04 second interval between each figure from the array with 40 figures. Finally, when you register the animation with the name 'Explosion' using the 'addAnimation' method, you are ready to use the animation.

(/src/sprite/Explosion.js)

```
......

Explosion.sharedExplosion = function () {
    var animFrames = [];
    var str = "";
    for (var i = 1; i < 40; i++) {
        str = "explosion_" + (i < 10 ? ("0" + i) : i) + ".png";
        var frame = cc.SpriteFrameCache.getInstance().getSpriteFrame(str);
        animFrames.push(frame);
    }
    var animation = cc.Animation.create(animFrames, 0.04);
    cc.animationCache.addAnimation(animation, "Explosion");
};

......
```

Now, it is the step to use the animation you made. In Block Breaking game, as the ball hits a block, block is broken, and an explosion animation appears in its place. Therefore, in Block class, you use explosion animation in 'destroy' function which breaks the block. Explosion class representing the explosion becomes an object using the function called 'getOrCreateExplosion' in it.

(/src/sprite/Block.js)

```
......
destroy:function () {
        GAME.SCORE += this.scoreValue;
        GAME.BLOCKCOUNT--;
        var a = Explosion.getOrCreateExplosion();
        a.attr({
                x: this.x,
                y: this.y
        });
        ......
```

If you place the object that became alive as such in the place of the block using 'attr' method, you will see the explosion animation on the screen. If you add explosion sound effect which you will learn later, the game will be much more interesting. And if you erase the block and the explosion animation, you can have a great effect of breaking the block.

8. Sound

Sound is a very important effect in a game or a movie. Because, a good sound effect makes the game more interesting. We used an explosion animation to give more effect of block breaking in Block Breaking game, and if we add an explosion sound, it will give more reality.

In Cocos2d framework, we use sound by registering a music file as a resource and using audio engine object. Now, let's find out how to develop a sound through the example of Block Breaking explosion sound.

Music file is also a resource used in a game like a figure file, you define it in 'Resource' under 'config' folder. The sounds used in Block Breaking game are initial music, background music, button sound effect and explosion sound effect. Among the music files to use, save 'explodeEffect.mp3' file that corresponds to the explosion sound to a global variable named 's_explodeEffect_mp3'.

(/src/config/Resource.js)

```
var res = {

    ......

    s_buttonEffect_mp3 : 'res/Music/buttonEffet.mp3',

    s_explodeEffect_mp3 : 'res/Music/explodeEffect.mp3',

    ......
```

Now, let's try to use the registered explosion sound resource. The explosion sound is used together with the explosion animation when a block is broken in the game. Therefore, in destroy function which corresponds to an explosion in Block class that corresponds to a block, use a method called PlayEffect of AudioEngine to play the explosion music file.

(/src/sprite/Block.js)

```
……
destroy:function () {
      GAME.SCORE += this.scoreValue;
      GAME.BLOCKCOUNT--;
      var a = Explosion.getOrCreateExplosion();
      a.attr({
            x: this.x,
            y: this.y
      });
      if(GAME.SOUND){
            cc.audioEngine.playEffect(res.s_explodeEffect_mp3);
      }
……
```

But, if you look carefully, explosion sound is only played when 'GAME.SOUND' variable value is 'True'. What does it mean? Yes. You can turn on or off the sound in the game setting. If you turn off the sound, 'GAME.SOUND' variable value becomes 'False', and sound will not be played.

The game setting is managed in SettingLayer class. If you look at the program code, when you press the sound setting toggle menu, the setting is switched between 'On' and 'Off' value. Every time you press the menu, a function named 'onSoundControl' is run. Every time the function is run, 'GAME.SOUND' variable value toggles between 'True' and 'False'. Variable value set as such is used to manage whether to use sound in the game.

(/src/layer/SettingLayer.js)

```
......

cc.MenuItemFont.setFontName("Arial");

cc.MenuItemFont.setFontSize(26);

var item1 = cc.MenuItemToggle.create(

        cc.MenuItemFont.create("On"),

        cc.MenuItemFont.create("Off") );

item1.setCallback(this.onSoundControl );

var state = GAME.SOUND ? 0 : 1;

item1.setSelectedIndex(state);

......

onSoundControl:function(){

    GAME.SOUND = !GAME.SOUND;

......
```

Then, let's find out how to use the sound through the example of the background sound in the initial screen.

(/src/layer/SystemMenu.js)

```
......
if (GAME.SOUND) {

    cc.audioEngine.setMusicVolume(0.7);

    cc.audioEngine.playMusic(res.s_mainMainMusic_mp3, true);

}
......
```

The layer corresponding to the initial screen is 'SysMenu'. If you check the program code, the music is played only when the sound setting value is set to play the sound as the same as the case above. You can also see some more functions in addition to 'playMusic'method that plays the music file. To adjust the volume of the music, you use 'setMusicVolume', and to stop the music, you can see that 'stopMusic' is used. Other functions such as pause or resume can be used as necessary.

9. Effects

The next effect is not a new function, but is rather a new effect made by combining various actions. If you adequately utilize attributes of individual actions such as transparency, location, rotation, and size, and combine several actions, you can make a good novel effect. In Cocos2d framework, various effects are provided, so you can easily use them, but for the purpose of training, we will make one by ourselves here.

Both Brick Breaker and Garden Keeper game make and use flare effect with a strong lighting on the screen when the game starts. A strong effect at the beginning of a game makes the game more interesting.

Then, let me take a look at an example of an effect used in Garden Keeper game and explain the effect. As we design the game structure, we decided to gather the effects used in the game in 'effect' folder. In Garden Keeper game, flare effect is developed in Effect class.

To make a strong moving lighting effect, you first need to register the following figure file with lighting. After registering the figure file, make a moving effect using various actions.

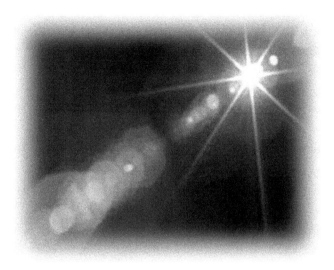

To use a figure file in a game, as the same as registering a figure file or a music file in the previous examples, define a figure file in a variable named 's_flare' in Resource class.

(/src/config/Resource.js)

```
var res = {

    ......

        s_flare : 'res/flare.jpg',

    ......
```

Next, we will make a function to show flare effect with the name of 'flareEffect' using the registered figure file. Create Sprite object from the registered figure file, and mix alpha values of the background and the current object with 'setBlendFunc' method of the created object to show the Sprite in half transparent state. And include the manipulated Sprite object in the screen with 'addChild' method.

Before showing a moving effect, change the flare figure object to a completely transparent state with 'opacity' attribute and locate it in rotated state outside the top left side. We will gradually enlarge the figure file, so reduce it to 20% of the original figure file size using 'scale' attribute.

(/src/layer/SystemMenu.js)

```
var flare = new cc.Sprite(res.s_flare);

.......

    flareEffect(flare, this, this.onNewGame);
}.bind(this));......
```

(/src/effect/Effect.js)

```
var flareEffect = function (flare, target, callback) {
    flare.stopAllActions();
    flare.setBlendFunc(cc.SRC_ALPHA, cc.ONE);
    flare.attr({
            x: -30,
            y: 297,
            visible: true,
            opacity: 0,
            rotation: -120,
            scale: 0.2
    });
    ......
```

Now, make various actions such as Fade, Scale, Ease, Move and Rotate that we learned above. We learned most of them, but CallFunc action is a new one. We call this a call back action, and it is used when you call a method from an action. The first parameter of a call back action is called selector which is a method to run, and the second is the target of a function run with the name of selectorTarget. If you look carefully the call back action named as 'onComplete', it is running the callback function which is received when you made flareEffect function. It will be explained a little later in the part calling flareEffect function.

(/src/effect/Effect.js)

```
......

var opacityAnim = cc.fadeTo(0.5, 255);

var opacDim = cc.fadeTo(1, 0);

var biggerEase = cc.scaleBy(0.7, 1.2, 1.2).easing(cc.easeSineOut());

var easeMove = cc.moveBy(0.5, cc.p(328, 0)).easing(cc.easeSineOut());

var rotateEase = cc.rotateBy(2.5, 90).easing(cc.easeExponentialOut());

var bigger = cc.scaleTo(0.5, 1);

var onComplete = cc.callFunc(callback, target);

var killflare = cc.callFunc(function () {

    this.parent.removeChild(this,true);

}, flare);

......
```

If you made various actions, now you can run the actions by adequately combining them and using runAction. You already learned how to use a sequence to run several actions sequentially.

(/src/effect/Effect.js)

```
flare.runAction(cc.sequence(opacityAnim, biggerEase, opacDim,
                            killflare, onComplete));

flare.runAction(easeMove);

flare.runAction(rotateEase);

flare.runAction(bigger);

......
```

So far, we analyzed effect function flareEffect which makes a flare effect. Now, let's use the effect. We decided to use flare effect in the initial screen when you start a new game, so let's take a look at the code making the corresponding menu.

(/src/layer/SystemMenu.js)

```
    var newGame = new cc.MenuItemSprite(newGameNormal,
                       newGameSelected, newGameDisabled, function () {
            this.onButtonEffect();

            flareEffect(flare, this, this.onNewGame);
        }.bind(this));

    ......
```

If you press the menu starting a new game, it will call flareEffect. When you call a function, the third parameter 'this.onNewGame' is a method starting a new game. 'this.onNewGame' method sent to flareEffect function is run after showing all the effects with the previously described call back action named onComplete. That is, if you select a menu to start a new game, it will move to a new game screen after running all effects of flareEffect function.

10. Transitions

We made an effect of screen transition using various actions. But if you can develop the screen transition easily without complex code, it will be much easier to make a game. Such various effects shown when a screen is converted are called transition. Cocos2d framework provides transition functions that can easily make great screen transitions.

Then, let's take a look at the transition in Garden Keeper game. In the initial menu screen, if you press 'Option' button, it moves to a new screen to change the game settings. If you give an effect of slowly dimming down and dimming up again, it will improve the reality of the game. We call the effect of dimming down and up a Fade effect. In the example game, it shows an interesting effect of dimming down and up the screen to convert to a new screen in the transition between the two screens using Fade transition as in the following figure.

We would like to look at the function to press a button in the initial menu screen before we go into the transition. To use the menu button, you need to register figure file to display the menu. We will register the following figure file with the name of 's_menu' using Resource class like other resources.

(/src/config/Resource.js)

```
var res = {

......

    s_menu : 'res/menu.png',

......
```

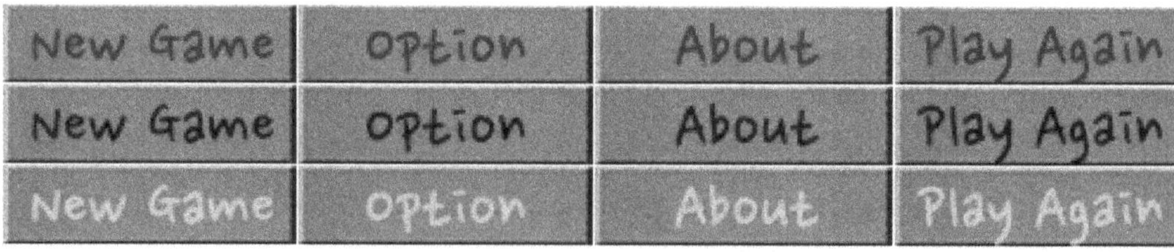

New Game	Option	About	Play Again
New Game	Option	About	Play Again
New Game	Option	About	Play Again

You registered the figure resource, and let's use it in the game. Menu figure file has 12 buttons in one file. We will designate territory and use it as menu button image by cutting the desired part. Here, to develop 'Option' button, we will cut 3 images to make a Sprite. The reason for using 3 images for one button is to express differently among the images of normal image, the image when the button is selected, and the image when the button is deactivated. Then, you can show the effect of the color of the letters of the button when the corresponding menu is selected in the game.

Shall we look at the program code? Designate the locations of the 3 button images and make them Sprite objects. And use 'MenuItemSprite' class to make the button menu. Register the 3 image Sprite objects, and designate function named 'onSettings' which is run when the menu is selected.

(/src/layer/SystemMenu.js)

```
......

var gameSettingsNormal = new cc.Sprite(res.s_menu,
                                cc.rect(126, 0, 126, 33));
var gameSettingsSelected = new cc.Sprite(res.s_menu,
                                cc.rect(126, 33, 126, 33));
var gameSettingsDisabled = new cc.Sprite(res.s_menu,
                                cc.rect(126, 33 * 2, 126, 33));

......

var gameSettings = new cc.MenuItemSprite(gameSettingsNormal,
                    gameSettingsSelected, gameSettingsDisabled,
                    this.onSettings, this);

......
```

Now, it is time to check the function to run when the menu item is selected. Make the Scene class to make a new screen as an object and register the game setting screen SettingsLayer object here. And register the Scene to director. We looked at the usage of 'runScene' method in the previous chapter of 'framework structure'.

Then, shall we start to develop transition function now? But, for some reason, we cannot see various actions or logics to develop the function. Only a method named 'TransitionFade' wraps the game setting screen Scene object.

Yes. Just by using a method provided by the framework, you can develop a great transition function. The number '1.2' in the method means the time to run the transition.

(/src/layer/SystemMenu.js)

```
......

onSettings:function (pSender) {

    this.onButtonEffect();

    var scene = new cc.Scene();

    scene.addChild(new SettingsLayer());

    cc.director.runScene(new cc.TransitionFade(1.2, scene));

},
```

When you make a game, there are figures used repeatedly in the background screen. If you make and repeatedly use small figure pieces from the pattern of the figures with the same sizes and the shapes, you can reduce the memory usage compared to using a big background figure. Tilemap concept is made from such idea. Tilemap is making a big figure of 'map' form by adequately positioning 'tile' which is a small figure pattern file used repeatedly.

We will also use a game example for better understanding. In Garden Keeper game, sparrows keep flying in the sky background. If you make figures of sparrows flying as a certain pattern and position them regularly, you can reduce the memory usage in a game.

Let's make 'tile' which is the figure pattern of the sparrows. If you show one sparrow repeatedly, it may become too boring. Therefore, making and using adequate number of sparrows will make a natural scene even if you show them repeatedly. We will make a pattern of flying sparrows as in the following figure. And we will save the figure file as the name of 'sparrow.png'.

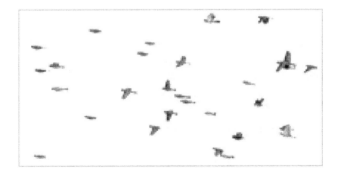

Now, we will make a big 'map' using the 'tile' which is a figure pattern of sparrow group. In Garden Keeper game, sparrows shall fly naturally, so you need to position them adequately. Compose a big background of 5 x 3 rectangular grid. And position the sparrow group figure pattern only in 3 regions as in the following figure. Leave the remaining space as a transparent space.

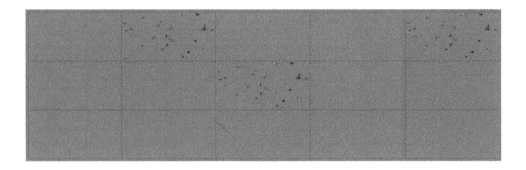

You need to make a file to save the tilemap composition information. In Cocos2d framework, save the tilemap information in a XML file using TMX extension. Shall we look at the contents a moment? Register 'sparrow.png' which is the sparrow group figure pattern file we made above. And declare 5 x 3 rectangular grid in the layer you use. You probably understand up to this point, but you will not be able to understand the tile arrangement information just by looking at the code since it is encoded in the data tag. So when you make a TMX file, you use an exclusive GUI based tilemap editor. There are already various open source based editors, so you can easily make the TMX file.

(/res/backGround.tmx)

```xml
<?xml version="1.0" encoding="UTF-8"?>

......

<image source="sparrow.png" width="200" height="100"/>
  </tileset>
  <layer name="Tile Layer 1" width="5" height="3">
    <data encoding="base64" compression="zlib">
      eJxjYGBgYGRAAFxsbAAAAMAABA==
    </data>

......
```

TMX file is a resource same as figure or music file, so you need to register it in Resource class. Save the TMX file in a variable named 's_backGround'.

(/src/config/Resource.js)

```
var res = {

......

    s_backGround : 'res/backGround.tmx',

......
```

Then, you are ready, so use the tilemap in the program. To register and use a tilemap in a program, use 'TMXTiledMap' class. Put tilemap object in a variable named '_backTileMap'. And make it move by 150 pixels for 3 seconds. It will look like sparrows flying.

(/src/layer/GameLayer.js)

```
......

this._backTileMap = new cc.TMXTiledMap(res.s_backGround);

this.addChild(this._backTileMap, -7);

this._backTileMapWidth = this._backTileMap._getMapWidth() *
                        this._backTileMap._getTileWidth();

......

this._backTileMapWidth -= 150;

this._backSky.runAction(cc.moveBy(3, cc.p(-20, 0)));

this._backTileMap.runAction(cc.moveBy(3, cc.p(-150, 0)));

this.schedule(this.movingBackground, 3);

......
```

And then, use scheduler to repeat the sparrows flying motion. If you look at the program code, you can easily guess that 'movingBackground' function has that role.

γ

Interesting

Game

Production

A re you curious about the history of games? We cannot pinpoint the period of the beginning of the games, but they say that portable games similar to chess appears in the ancient Egypt civilization. Perhaps the games for the leisure time advanced along with the start of the human civilization.

Then, shall we go back to the beginning of the digital games? It also seems difficult to mark a clear line exactly for the origin of the digital games. When the computers were developed, there were various tries to make the digital games. Among those, many people acknowledge 'Tennis for Two', a 2 player tennis game made by Dr. Willy Higgingbotham in U.S in 1958, as the fist digital video game.

The true matrix of the video games was a game called 'Space War', developed in 1961 by Steve Russel and his colleagues in MIT. It was an important milestone becoming the foundations for many game frameworks and the development philosophy afterwards.

This game has another contribution to the history of the games. It provided a vision to Nolan Bushnell, who is called 'the Father of Video Games' today, and established a company called ATARI which contributed greatly to the popularization of the video games.

A vision of a young man encounters the efforts of many people and makes the history of the games as we know now.

1. Structure of a Game

I am planning to use JavaScript, Cocos2d-JS and the programs, that you learned so far, to make an interesting game. Before developing the functions of the game, if you go through the works of designing a solid structure of the game, the development followed will be easier and consistent user environment will be provided. We will make two games using the principles of Mathematics and Physics. If each game has different structure, there will be less common parts and more development works, and it may cause confusions to the users playing the games. Therefore, we wish to unify the structure of the games into the same form as much as possible.

The structure of the game we are making is an example provided by Cocos2d-JS framework, and it is modified for convenience based on the structure of 'Moon Warriors' game. The names of the classes were made similar as much as possible, so that it can help you learn 'Moon Warriors' game in the future.

Let's list up the structure of the game based on the user screens. As the user starts the game, there is 'Loader' that makes you move to the initial screen. Sometimes, if it takes time to start a game, it shows program loading screen, but the loading screen may be omitted.

The initially displayed screen when the game is loaded is 'Main Menu'. We can choose from 3 choices in the initial screen. The first choice is 'New Game' menu which starts a new game, and the second choice is 'Option' menu that adjusts sound volume or difficulty of the game. The third choice is 'About' menu that shows the introduction and description of the game.

According to the choice of the user, you can move to three different screens. Among those screens, if you moved to 'Option' or 'About' screen, there is 'Go Back' menu that enables you to return to 'Main Menu'. Also in 'New Game' screen that executes the game, we will make a function to return to 'Main Menu' in the middle of the game when the user wishes. When a task of the game is completed, level will increase, 'New Game' is open in a new level, and the game continues. If you did not complete the task of the game, you move to 'Game Over' screen, and if you choose 'Play Again' menu there, you can move to 'Game Play' screen and play a new game.

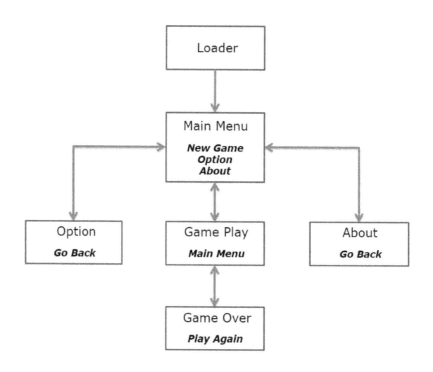

If necessary, you can make a screen managing the score rankings, and you can also make a menu to move from 'Game Over' screen to 'Main Menu'. Important thing here is making a consistent game structure. If you use the same game structure, when you make a new game, you can reuse many parts of the existing program, and the users can also enjoy the game with more familiarity.

We will use same screen flows for both 'Brick Breaker' and "Garden Keeper' games. I used same names of JavaScript files for both projects. For example, I used 'SystemMenu.js' for 'Main Menu' stage. Let us see a screen structure of 'Brick Braker' first.

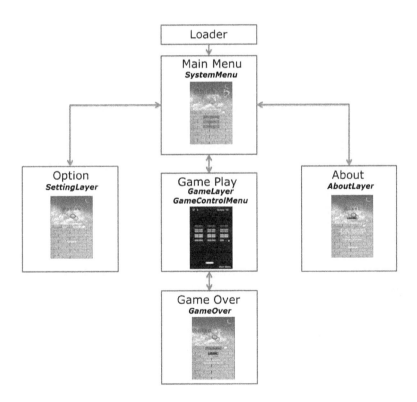

Now we can compare it to a structure of Garden Keeper game. Both are exactly same! Yes, we will use same structure for two sample games. It will bring us efficiency, code resusability and other merits for development

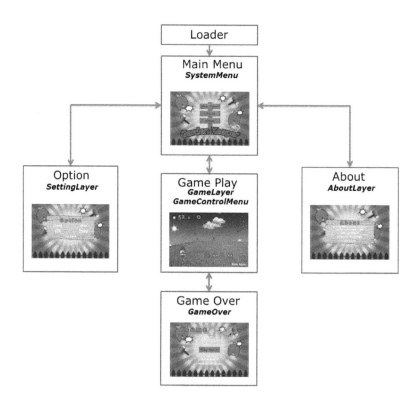

Now, let's list up the structure of the game in terms of the program source code management. If you list up the program source code in a similar form, it is easy to manage and to expand. Such management units are also managed with the concept called package. If you manage the program source codes with a consistent unit, when you add or modify according to the characteristics of the game, the trace and the management will be easier.

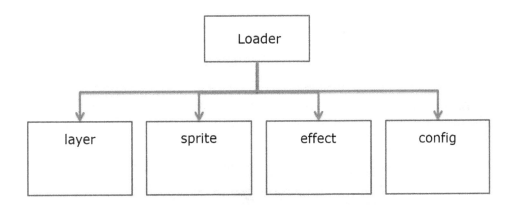

We are planning to manage the program in four units. The first unit is the layer composing the game screens that we learned above. It is the place to store the program source codes related to the screens such as 'Main Menu', 'Game Play', 'Game Over', etc. The second unit is the place to store Sprites, which are the independent moving units such as characters, etc. We will study the concept of Sprite later in detail. The next is the unit called 'effect' which manages various screen effects, and the last unit is the place called 'config' which stores a program managing various settings of the game.

You don't have to worry now even if you don't know the details. You just need to understand that consistent management of the game structure will be efficient. You will be naturally familiar with the game structure as you make the game according to the game structure.

2. Planning Brick Breaker

Now, let's plan the first game. It will be in order that the game program shall be completed through planning and designing, but for easier understanding, let's summarize what kind of a game we are making by looking at the screens of the completed game.

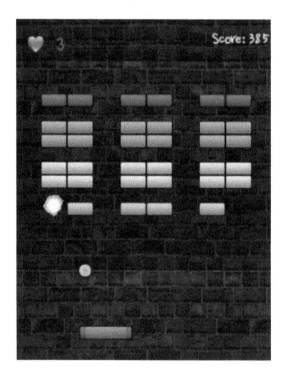

The game we are making is Brick Breaker game, which is very familiar with us. You move the bar to hit the moving ball, and the ball hits the blocks until all the blocks disappear. If you do not receive the moving ball and the ball passes the bar, your life

141

decreases one by one. I hope it is a game you played at least once, and even if you never played it before, it is a simple structure, and you will be able to understand soon.

When you make a game, it is better to summarize and express the game with the simplest sentence. Then you can define the core elements of the game in simple terms. Let's define our Brick Breaker game.

The game player moves the bar to hit the moving ball.

If the ball collides with the block, the block disappears. When all the blocks are removed, the task is completed.

.

Then, let's define the characters and the roles in the game. In the game, there are bar, ball, blocks, and explosions. The characters appearing in the game are made as the form of Sprite. You don't have to worry for the unfamiliar term. You will naturally learn it in the process of learning the program.

	Bar (Bar.js): It is a tool for the game player to move left and right to hit the ball. When the ball hits the bar, it is reflected to the opposite direction.
	Ball (Ball.js): It is reflected when it hits the bar, wall, or block. When the ball hits a block and the block is destroyed, the score increases.

	Block (Block.js): It is destroyed when it is hit by the ball, and the ball is reflected. Every time the block is destroyed, score increases, and when all the blocks are destroyed, the game stage is completed.
	Explosion (Explosion.js): It is the effect screen appearing when the ball hits the block, and it is an animation shown with an explosion sound effect.

Now, let's list up the screens to develop. As some of you may have already guessed, the screens will be developed as the form of Layers. Also for the Layers, we will study later in detail from the concept to the program development. Since we already defined the structure of a general game, so let's list up the necessary screens one by one according to the structure.

	Main Menu(SystemMenu.js): It is the initial screen of the game, and you can select one from three menus, 'Game Play', 'Option', or 'About' and move to that screen.

	Option(SettingsLayer.js): There is a menu to adjust the sound and difficulty of the game, and you can return to ' Main Menu'
	About(AboutLayer.js): You can view the information about the game, and there is 'Go Back' menu that can return to 'Main Menu'.
	Game Play(GameLayer.js, GameControlMenu.js): It is the screen displayed when the game is in progress, and the two Layers, game Layer and the Layer with a button to return to 'Main Menu', are overlapped.
	Game Over(GameOver.js): When the game is over, it displays the score, and when you select 'Play Again' menu, you can restart the game.

So far, as we listed up the characters and screens, you can easily develop most of the program. The remaining parts are the program start function, effect expression function, or parts to define the settings of the game.

Next, let's design the game based on the planned contents of the characters and the screens.

3. Design Brick Breaker

Now, it is time to design the game. If you thought of the characters and the screens of the game through the previous planning stage, the designing is the specific designing of the program structure before the actual coding. Now, you may think it is a waste of time or unnecessary to go through the planning or designing stages, but eventually, it is an important process to reduce the development time and to increase the completeness of the program.

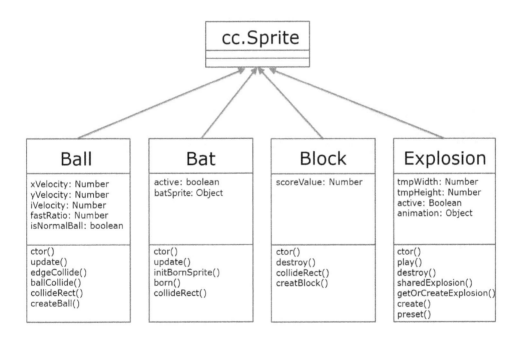

To design a game program, we will use UML(Unified Modeling Language). To describe UML in easy terms, it is a graphic language to easily document the analysis of the program and the contents of the design. There are various forms of diagrams in UML, and we will use Class Diagram to structurally list up the class concept Sprites.

As thinking of the planned contents again, we will design the characters in the game as Sprites. All of the four classes, ball, bar, block, and explosion, inherit Sprite class. In another words, the general functions for a character to be equipped with are developed in the Sprites, which are the parents, so they are inherited and used as they are, and the programmer only needs to develop the functions unique to each class. It is the characteristics and also the advantage of an object oriented programming.

In UML class diagram, you first write the name of the class, and in the box above, you list up the variables used in the class. And then, you write the methods used in the following box.

If you look at the contents of the Ball class which represents the ball, you will have much easier understanding of the four classes.

In Ball class, there are variables called xVelocity, yVelocity, and iVelocity, which represent the x and y of the ball, and the speed increase/decrease. If you increase the difficulty of the game, a faster ball appears, and you also make a variable called fastRatio which represents the speed of the faster ball. And you also define a variable called isNormalBall, which classifies the created Ball object into normal ball or faster ball.

Let's list up the various functions of the ball as methods. First, there is constructor function 'ctor()', which is executed when Ball object is created. You also need a function called 'update()' that defines the change of the motion of the ball as time goes. You also need the methods, 'edgeCollide()', which defines function when the ball collides with the wall, and 'ballCollide()' that composes the logic when the ball hits the bar. Also define a function 'collideRect()' to define the collision range of the ball. And, if you define 'createBall()', which is used to make a ball from outside, you can use the ball in the game.

Now, let's define the 'Layer' to make the functions of the screen. We will also express the 6 Layers planned previously as UML class diagrams. All screen classes also inherit the parent class called Layer.

Among those, let's look at SystemMenu class which expresses the initial screen.

You only need one variable '_ball' that expresses the floating balls in the initial screen. You need to develop 'ctor()' and 'init()' method which is executed initially when it is created as an object. We previously said as we defined the functions, that there are 3 menus in the initial screen, and when you press 'New Game' menu, 'onNewGame()' function is executed, when you press 'Option' button, 'onSettings()' method is executed, and when you select 'About' menu, 'onAbout()' is executed. We will also define 'update()' function which changes continuously according to the schedule and 'onButtonEffect()' which makes the sound effect. When you define 'scene()' method which includes the Layer in the Scene, all functions are completed.

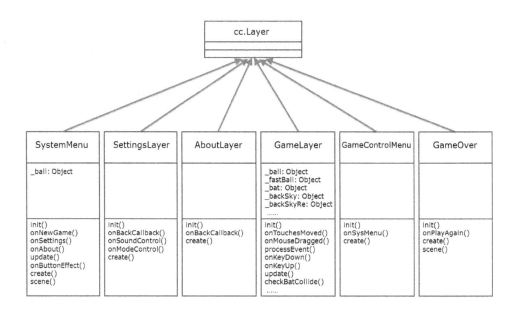

We looked at each of Sprite and Layer, so you can calmly think and define the rest with the same method. It may be difficult and not familiar now, but if you repeat the process of planning, designing and actually coding the program, and when you become familiar, you will find yourself who already became a good programmer.

4. Control Velocity

Now, we will have the time to understand the major logics of the first game Brick Breaker. We already have studied essential skills of Cocos2d-JS in the last section. So, I would like to explain major algorithm, principle and logics of the game in following chapters. It is better to understand some core Mathematics and Physics logic to make good games. There are some principle of Mathematics and Physics. Don't too much worry about it. When you study priciples of Matha and Physics using game samples, you will understand the imporetance of science hidden in a game.

The first thing to learn is to understand the concept of velocity hidden in a game. In Brick Breaker game, the ball makes an ideal speed motion. There is no friction or external resistance such as wind, and it keeps moving in a uniform speed. It is like an object moving in zero gravity state space according to the size of the force and direction. In general mode, blue ball makes speed motion, and when the game is in hard mode, another red ball with faster speed appears.

You already learned enough previously, but let's review about the concept of speed and acceleration. We will simply review and go on.

An object making a motion for certain time t with a uniform speed v_0 is called uniform motion. And the motion with added speed a during a unit time is called an accelerated motion. We explained the relationship for displacement representing the moving distance in acceleration, speed, and physics in uniform motion and accelerated motion using a table.

	Uniform Movement	Acceleration Movement
Acceleration a	0	a
Velocity v	v_0	$v_0 + at$
Displacement S	$v_0 t$	$v_0 t + \dfrac{1}{2}at^2$

As in uniform motion, displacement, which is the moving distance, is proportional to the movement time, and as in the left side graph, you can easily get it with the value of multiplying the speed and the time.

But the method of getting the displacement in accelerated motion is a little complex. First, let's understand the meaning of acceleration. Acceleration a a means the amount of speed change Δv during the unit time t. To express it in a formula, it is $a = \frac{\Delta v}{t}$. If you modify the formula a little bit, the increased speed Δv can be calculated by multiplying acceleration a and time t.

In an accelerated motion, as in the right side graph, you can see that the displacement S is composed of the sum of a rectangle multiplying initial speed v_0 and time t and a triangle $\frac{1}{2}at^2$, which is the multiplication of at, which is the multiplication of speed change Δv, that is the acceleration and the time.

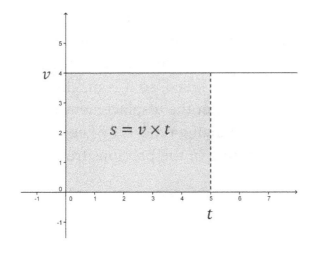

The displacement in the uniform movement

$$S = v_0 t$$

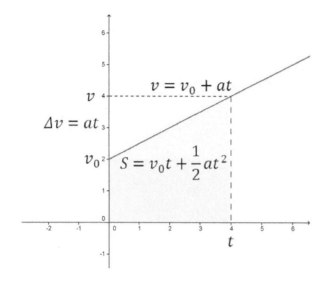

The displacement in the acceleration movement

$$S = v_0 t + \frac{1}{2} a t^2$$

Then, let's go back to Block Breaking game and find out the speed motion of the ball in the program. The program code related to the motion of the ball is developed in Ball class.

First, declare a variable with the name of 'xVelocity' and 'yVelocity' meaning x and y axis speed. And, set the initial value as '100' for now. Keep calculating and axis displacement in 'update' function which is run at every frame to change the location. The ball moves in a uniform speed, so it is making a uniform motion. Therefore, you can get the displacement S by multiplying the speed v_0 and the changing time t. By keep adding the displacement value to the location in the previous frame, you can get the changed location.

(/src/sprite/Ball.js)

```
var Ball = cc.Sprite.extend({

  xVelocity:100,

  yVelocity:100,

  ......

  ctor:function (isNormal) {

    ......

    this.scheduleUpdate();

  },

  update:function (dt) {

          var x = this.x, y = this.y;

          this.x += this.xVelocity * dt;

          this.y += this.yVelocity * dt;

  ......
```

Next, let's find out about the motion of the red ball. Red ball has faster speed than blue ball, but it also makes a uniform motion. Therefore, you can get the changing motion with the same uniform motion formula.

The program code to set the red ball with faster speed is as follows.

When you create Ball class object, if you set 'isNormal' parameter value as 'True', a blue ball is created, and if you set it as 'False', a red ball is created as an object.

(/src/sprite/Ball.js)

```
var Ball = cc.Sprite.extend({
```

```
xVelocity:100,

yVelocity:100,

iVelocity:20,

fastRatio:1.5,

isNormalBall:true,

ctor:function (isNormal) {

        this.isNormalBall = isNormal;

        var ballPic = this.isNormalBall ? "Ball.png" : "fastBall.png";

        this._super("#"+ballPic);

        var xLevelVelocity = this.xVelocity+ this.iVelocity*GM.LEVEL;

        var yLevelVelocity = this.yVelocity+ this.iVelocity*GM.LEVEL;

        this.xVelocity = this.isNormalBall ? xLevelVelocity :

                                xLevelVelocity * this.fastRatio;

        this.yVelocity = this.isNormalBall ? yLevelVelocity :

                                yLevelVelocity * this.fastRatio;

......
```

When you complete a task of a game, you go up to the next level, and the increased speed value is set in 'iVelocity' variable. Every time it becomes a new level, it is set to be increased by 20. And the degree of faster speed of a red ball compared to a blue ball is set in 'fastRatio' variable. Here, it is set as faster by 1.5 times.

Now, you checked the principle of the speed motion hidden in the game and the developed code. If you follow the remaining contents one by one, you will also be interested in Mathematics and Physics as well as the game.

5. Collision detection

In this chapter, we will learn about the collision, which is an important concept in game and Physics. Many games use the collision. Not only in Brick Breaking and Garden Keeper game that we use, but also in Invader, Billiard, Tank game, etc., or perhaps in most of the games, collision is used. A ball hitting the wall and bouncing is also a phenomenon of a collision, mole hit by the hammer, airplane hit by a bomb and exploding are also a phenomenon of a collision.

First, let's review the basic Physics knowledge about collision.

One of the important concepts in collision is the law of conservation of momentum. Both the object imposing the shock and the object receiving the shock have momentum changes, and the sums of the momentum of the two objects are equal before and after the collision.

Then, let's list up as a formula. The times of contact at the collision of the two objects are the same, so the impulses received by the two objects are the same, and the directions are the opposite. The value A which is the multiple of the weight of the ball m_A before the collision and the speed v_A is the momentum. You can also calculate the momentum of the hitting ball B with the same method. When the two balls collide, the speed of one ball will decrease and the speed of the other ball will increase. The momentum of the ball A after the collision is the multiple of the ball's weight m_A and speed after the collision $v_A{}'$. If you reflect the speed of ball B after the collision, you can get the momentum. Momentum of each of the ball A and B have changes before and after the collision, but you can see that the sum of the momentums of the two objects is not changed before and after the collision.

$$m_A v_A + m_B v_B = m_A v_A{'} + m_B v_B{'}$$

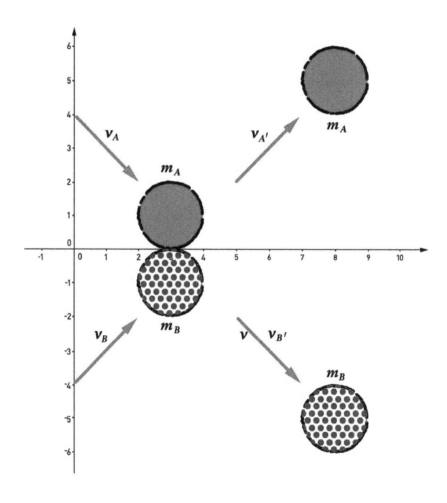

Game such as Billiard is a typical example of using the law of conservation of momentum. When a ball runs and hits another ball, speed and direction are changed, and if there is no external element such as friction, they will move according to the law of conservation of momentum. The speed of the first ball will decrease after the collision, and the speed of the ball hit by the first ball will increase.

We will understand about the collision and motion through Block Breaking game. But, Block Breaking game is a somewhat unrealistic game. There is no external variable to reduce the speed such as friction on the surface where the ball runs, and most of all, the speed of the ball does not change at all after the collision. But, the direction after the collision becomes the opposite.

Then, let's look at the program code of Block Breaking game and see how the principle of collision is developed in the game. The function to change the direction when the ball collides with the wall or bar is developed in Ball class.

Let's take a look at the contents of 'edgeCollide' function that defines the action when the ball hits the wall and 'ballCollide' function that defines the function when the ball hits the bar.

(/src/Sprite/Ball.js)

```
......
edgeCollide:function () {
        var x = this.x, y = this.y;
        var ballWidth = this.width;
        var ballHeight = this.height;
        if (x < ballWidth/2 ||
            x > (g_sharedGameLayer.screenRect.width - ballWidth/2)) {
①       this.xVelocity *= -1;

        }
        if (y < 0) {
②          this.yVelocity *= -1;

            GAME.LIFE--;

            g_sharedGameLayer._bat.active = false;

            var batX = g_sharedGameLayer._bat.x;

            var batY = g_sharedGameLayer._bat.y;

            this.x = batX;

            this.y = batY + 30;

        }
```

```
    if (y > (g_sharedGameLayer.screenRect.height - ballHeight/2)) {
  ③    this.yVelocity *= -1;

    }

},

ballCollide:function () {
  ④    this.yVelocity *= -1;

......
```

① Changing the direction in *x* axis occurs when the ball hits the wall on the left or right side. The location of the ball is recognized by the center of the ball, so you need to subtract by 'ballWidth/2' which corresponds to the radius of the ball.

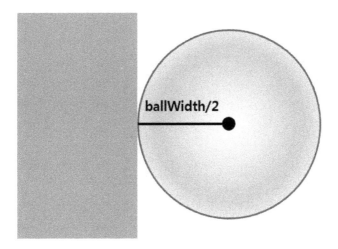

② The reason of changing the direction in y axis is because the ball passed the bar and reached the floor. In such case, the life of the game is decreased by 1, and a new ball appears 30 above in *y* axis from the bar to start again.

③ Here, the reason that the ball changes the direction in y axis is because it hit the ceiling. You also need to change the direction of the ball at the location of subtracting the radius of the ball from the height of the game screen.

④ When the ball hits the bar, you need to change the location of the ball in *y* axis direction again.

6. Planning Garden Keeper

You already planned the first game, so the second is expected to be much easier. Also for this game, before studying the contents of the plan, we recommend you to run the completed game first. Playing the game itself will be a big help to understand the contents. After finishing the second tutorial, you will have the skills to be able to plan a game from the beginning without looking at a completed game example.

The 'Garden Keeper' game that we are planning to make is a game to throw an object and to hit the target with a parabolic trajectory. It is also a game very familiar to us as the Brick Breaker game. It is also a good example with a lot of mathematics and physics principles such as speed, trigonometric function, parabolic motion, etc.

The story of the game is like this. Keeper tries to keep the garden beautiful. But the Moles come to the garden and try to ruin the garden, and the Keeper defeats the Moles with hammers. When the game starts, you have to defeat the set number of Moles in certain time period. Every time you defeat a Mole, the score increases. We will again define the core of the game in simple text to make simple definition of the core elements of the game.

Game player throws the Keeper's hammer to hit the Mole in the garden. If you hit the Mole with the hammer, Mole will disappear and the score increases. If you hit certain number of Moles in the set period of time, your task is completed.

.

Again, let's define the roles of the characters in the game. There are hammers, Keeper, Moles, and target marks in the game. We already learned that the characters in the game are made as the form of Sprites during the programming. Now, let's define the characters to be made as the Sprites.

	Hammer(Hammer.js): It is the object that Keeper throws, and when the hammer flies and hit the Mole, the Mole will disappear, and the score increases.

	Keeper(Keeper.js): It is the guardian of the garden, and when the Mole appears, it is the main character who adjusts the strength according to the distance and throws the hammer to drive out the Moles.
	Mole(Mole.js): It is the pests that ruin the garden, and when it disappears when it is hit by the hammer thrown by the Keeper. If you hit certain number of Moles with hammer in the set period of time, the game stage is completed.
	Target(Target.js): It only appears when the game is in beginner's mode, and when the Keeper adjusts the strength, it plays the role of a helper by marking the expected impact point in advance.

You have defined the characters in the game, so we will list up the game screens next. As explained above, the game screens will be developed as the forms of Layers. Since we are making a new game, let's list up the necessary screens one by one with a fresh mind.

	Main Menu(SysMenu.js): It is the initial screen of the game, and you can select one among the 3 menus, 'Game Play',

	'Option', and 'About', to move to the corresponding screen.
	Option(SettingsLayer.js): It has a menu to adjust the sound and the difficulty of the game, and you can also return to ' Main Menu'.
	About(AboutLayer.js): You can view the information about the game, and there is 'Go Back' menu that can return to 'Main Menu'.
	Game Play(GameLayer.js, GameControlMenu.js): It is the screen displayed when the game is in progress, and the two Layers, game Layer and the Layer with a button to return to 'Main Menu', are overlapped.
	Game Over(GameOver.js): When the game is over, it displays the score, and when you select 'Play Again' menu, you can restart the game.

But it is a little odd. We listed up the game screens with a fresh mind, but they are somewhat familiar to us. Actually, they are exactly the same as the screen definitions as in the first game. Do you now understand the reasons to design the common game structure and started making the game? Even if you make a new game, if we use the same game structure, many parts in the programming can be use them as they are. You only need to develop the new functions of the game.

7. Designing Garden Keeper

Now it is the time to design the second game. Remember the above listed game planning well and improve your ability to design a game.

We will also use ULM class diagram to define the Sprites, which are the classes of the game. Let's move the characters listed up in the game planning to the Sprites and list up the necessary variables and methods one by one.

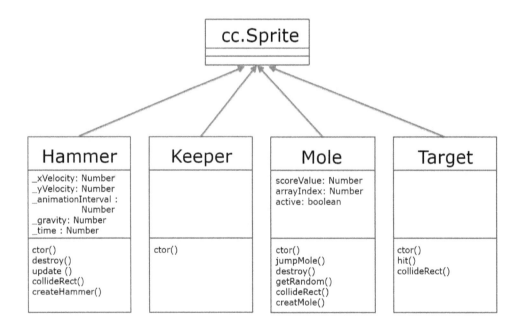

Also in this game, all the character classes inherit the Sprite classes. According to the characteristics of the object oriented programming, the general functions for a character to be equipped with are developed in the Sprites, which are the parents, they are used as they are, and the programmer only needs to develop the functions unique to each class.

Among the four classes, we will improve our game designing ability by looking at the contents of Hammer class.

In Hammer class, there are variables, '_xVelocity' and '_yVelocity' which represent x and y axis speed of the flying hammer. The hammer makes a parabola and makes the acceleration of gravity action, so we make a variable '_gravity' corresponding to the acceleration of gravity and a variable '_animationInterval' which represents the change time of the acceleration motion. Finally, we add a variable '_time' which represents the time to calculate the changes in y axis. You already learned mathematics and physics principles, so I think you already guessed what they are. You don't have to worry even if you do not remember them. You will later learn how to make the Hammer parabola motion program using mathematics and physics formulas.

Let's list up various functions of the Hammer as methods. First, there is constructor function 'ctor()' executed when Hammer object is created. We develop the function to be executed when the Hammer disappears in 'destroy()' method. We need a function 'update()' to define the motion change of the Hammer according to the time change. We also define a function 'collideRect()' to define the range of the Hammer's collision. And if you define 'createHammer()' used when a Hammer is created externally, we are ready to make Hammer class.

Following the characters, let's also define the classes making the functions of the screens. Again, let's express the previously planned 6 Layers as UML class diagram.

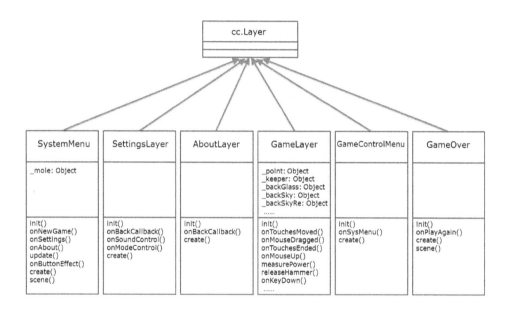

In the first game, we looked at SysMenu class which expressed the initial screen, but this time, we will look at the last screen of the game, GameOver. You don't need any variables. The first method to develop is 'ctor()' and 'init()' which is executed in the beginning when it is created as an object. In the initial screen, we defined that there are 3 menus, and again in the last screen, there is only one menu, 'Play Again' which starts the game again. If you press 'Play Again' menu, 'onPlayAgain()' function is executed. When you define 'scene()' method which includes the Layer in the Scene, all functions are completed.

If you take a look the remaining Layers calmly, you can easily understand them.

So far, we defined and designed the functions for the two games. We recommend you to first define the game structure and put a lot of effort and time into designing the functions. Then the game's completeness will be improved and you can become a good programmer.

8. Falling Motion

Shall we go back to the story of Galilei for a moment? We remember the Falling Theory completed by the falling experiment of Galilei. Let's think about the free-fall motion among them. Free-fall is a motion of a stopped object falling toward the direction of the center of the earth. The reason for an object falling toward the direction of the center of the earth is the force of the earth pulling objects.

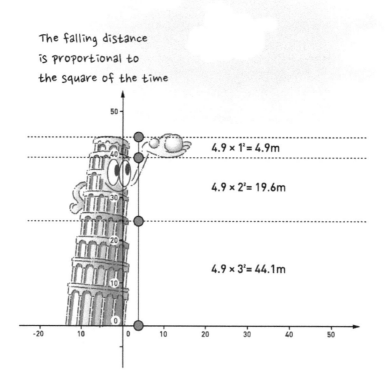

The falling distance is proportional to the square of the time

$4.9 \times 1^2 = 4.9\text{m}$

$4.9 \times 2^2 = 19.6\text{m}$

$4.9 \times 3^2 = 44.1\text{m}$

Let's imagine that Galilei dropped an iron ball from the Leaning Tower of Pisa. We will assume that the height of the Leaning Tower of Pisa is $55m$ and the iron ball is dropped from the top of the tower. If you let go of the iron ball, it makes a free-fall for about $5m$ during the first 1 second, and then it falls about $20m$ during the next 1 second. By 3 seconds after the drop, it falls about $45m$.

To get the displacement, which is the distance of the falling of the iron ball, let's think of the accelerated motion formula which we learned above. When you think of the accelerated motion that you learned above, you will understand.

$$S = v_0 t + \frac{1}{2} a t^2$$

In the falling motion, we will simply make a formula using known values. The object was at a still state in the beginning, so the initial speed v_0 is 0. And the acceleration of gravity, which is the force pulling toward the center of the earth, a is about 9.8m / s². If you input the two values, the formula becomes simple. If you simplify the formula to get the falling distance S of an object in a free-fall motion, it is as the following formula.

$$S = 4.9t^2$$

Eventually, the distance of the fall of the iron ball is proportional to the square of time. It was much easier to understand when you simplify it as a free-fall situation.

We logically checked out the formula to get the displacement, which is the moving distance of the fall motion, so let's how to develop the fall motion in *y* axis direction in a game.

The fall motion in y axis direction in Garden Keeper is not a free-fall motion. In a parabola accelerated motion, there is y axis direction speed v_y, and acceleration is gravity acceleration g. Gravity acceleration is uniform in the earth, and it is about $9.8m / s^2$. But the gravity is toward the center of the earth, which is the opposite direction of y axis, so it will be expressed in a negative value. Then, let's get the fall motion in y axis direction in Garden Keeper as a formula.

$$s = v_y t - \frac{1}{2}gt^2$$

In Garden Keeper game, hammer motion is defined in Hammer class. First, declare variables defining *x* and *y* axis speed, gravity acceleration, and time, and substitute '9.8' to variable named '_gravity' meaning the gravity acceleration. Save the *x* and *y* axis speed received from the constructor, which is run when Hammer object is created, and time in the variable.

Now, it is time to look at the contents of 'update' function, which is run every time game animation frame is changed. Accumulate the time that changes every time frame is run and save it in '_time' variable which means time *t*. And arrange the program code according to the formula to get the displacement of *y* axis direction accelerated motion which is defined above.

(/src/sprite/Hammer.js)

```
var Hammer = cc.Sprite.extend({

  _xVelocity:0,

  _yVelocity:0,

  _animationInterval:1 / 60,

  _gravity:9.8,

  _time:0,

  ctor:function (xVelocity, yVelocity) {

    this._xVelocity = xVelocity;

    this._yVelocity = yVelocity;

  ......

  update:function (dt) {

    this._time = this._time + this._animationInterval;

    var xp = GAME.KEEPER.XPOSITION +  this._xVelocity * this._time;

    var yp = GAME.KEEPER.YPOSITION +  this._yVelocity *

            this._time - 0.5*this._gravity*Math.pow(this._time,2);

  ......
```

So far, we looked at the speed motion and the fall motion hidden in the game. From the next chapter, we will go out to explore more interesting principles of science such as vector, parabolic motion, trigonometrical function and collision.

9. Parabola Motion

In the above, we enjoyed the principles of science by looking at the speed motion and fall motion in the game. In this chapter, through more interesting parabolic motion, we will find out how Mathematics and Physics are applied to a game.

Let's go back to Garden Keeper game. If the gardener adjusts the force and throws the hammer, the hammer makes a parabola and flies toward the target.

We will look at the hammer flying animation and study the principle of the simulation predicting the vector, parabola motion and impact point.

Shall we review about the vector that we are learning for the first time for a moment? When you studied above about Mathematics and Physics, we explained the movement of the coordinates having size of force and direction as a vector. With the examples of tug-of-war, jet stream flying and a boat crossing a river, we understood the principle of the vector. If you want to review the concept, it may be a good choice to go back and study the chapter about the vector.

Since we decided to study the vector and the parabola motion, let's think of a new example. When a football player kicks a football high forward, the ball flies making a parabola. To find out about the principle of an ideal parabolic motion, we will assume that there is no external element such as wind or friction.

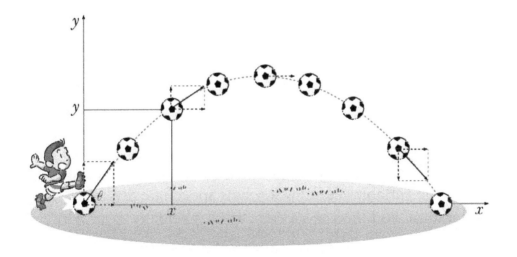

If you look at the motion of the ball in Physics terms, a new vector is created by combining the forces in x, y axis direction. While the motion in x axis direction is a uniform motion having only the force of throwing the object, the motion in y axis direction is an accelerated motion having both the initial throwing speed and gravity acceleration g. Gravity acceleration is uniform on earth, and it is about $9.8m / s^2$. But, gravity is toward the center of the earth, which is the opposite direction from y axis, so it will be expressed in negative number.

Let's list up the x, y axis direction motion used in the game in a table.

	x axis *Uniform Movement*	y axis *Acceleration Movement*
Acceleration a	0	$-g$
Velocity v	v_x	$v_y - gt$
Displacement S	$v_x t$	$v_y t - \dfrac{1}{2} gt^2$

Then, shall we check the motion of the hammer defined in Hammer class in Garden Keeper game? As explained above, declare the variables defining x, y axis speed, gravity acceleration, and time as '_xVelocity', '_yVelocity', '_gravity', and '_time'.

And complete the program code to get the displacement of x, y axis direction motion according to the above listed up Physics formula.

(/src/sprite/Hammer.js)

```
var Hammer = cc.Sprite.extend({
    _xVelocity:0,
    _yVelocity:0,
    _animationInterval:1 / 60,
    _gravity:9.8,
    _time:0,
    ......
    update:function (dt) {
        this._time = this._time + this._animationInterval;
        var xp = GAME.KEEPER.XPOSITION + this._xVelocity * this._time;
        var yp = GAME.KEEPER.YPOSITION + this._yVelocity *
                this._time - 0.5*this._gravity*Math.pow(this._time,2);
    ......
```

This time, let's make a more interesting function. If you set the setting of Garden Keeper game to easy mode, it shows the predicted impact point of the hammer as a target mark before the hammer is thrown. It will be much easier to play the game if we show the impact point in advance. It will be great if such function exists when you shoot a cannonball in a real combat. If there is a simulation function calculating the impact point before you shoot the cannonball, you will be able to easily suppress the enemy without wasting the cannonballs.

Then, let's use the parabolic motion formula to study the method to simulate the falling location of an object in advance. For the simulation, the most important thing is predicting the time for an object from starting to reach the target. There may be several methods to predict the flying time, but we will use the formula to get the displacement in y axis direction in the accelerated motion which we learned above. First, let's list up the formula to get the displacement in y axis direction.

$$S = v_y t - \frac{1}{2} g t^2$$

As we look carefully, the formula can be divided to two parts. The front part $v_y t$ is about the displacement by the speed in y axis direction. The rear part $\frac{1}{2} g t^2$ is about the displacement where the gravity acceleration occurs.

In Physics, as we study the velocity and the speed, we found out that the displacement S is different from the actual distance of the movement. The meaning of having 0 as the displacement in y axis direction is that the object left 0 location in y axis and returned to 0 location again.

That is, the location where the object is fired, made the parabolic motion, and falling on the ground is the location where displacement S becomes 0. If you use the formula to get displacement S in y axis direction, you can get the flying time t as $\frac{2v_y}{g}$ as follows.

$$S = 0 = v_y t - \frac{1}{2} g t^2$$

$$\frac{1}{2} g t^2 = v_y t$$

$$t = \frac{2 v_y}{g}$$

We will make a variable to get the flying time t, which the object flies, makes a parabolic motion, and arrives on the ground in Garden Keeper game. Set the name of the variable as 'timeToGround', and input the program code according to the formula.

(/src/layer/GameLayer.js)

```
......
measurePower:function( event ) {
  if( this._state == STATE_PLAYING ) {

    ......

    if(GAME.EASYMODE) {
      var timeToGround = 2 * this._deltaYvalue / this._gravity;
      var xpositionToGround = GAME.KEEPER.XPOSITION +
                    this._deltaXvalue * timeToGround ;

      ......

    this._target.attr({
      opacity: 255,
```

```
          x: xpositionToGround,

          y: GM.KEEPER.YPOSITION

     });

     ......
```

Since you calculated the predicted flying time t t, you can also predict the flying distance in x axis direction before you throw the object. Then, you can adjust the size of the force and simulate the flying distance of the object in advance to hit the target at once.

In Garden Keeper game, the predicted location of the hammer flying and falling is marked as a target. In easy mode, if you adjust the size of the force, the target will move, and if you fire when the target is on the mole, the hammer will hit the target.

We will make the predicted displacement flying in x axis direction as a variable called 'xpositionToGround'. The value can be calculated by multiplying x axis direction velocity '_deltaXvalue' and the predicted flying time 'timeToGround' as in the figure. The hammer is fired from the location of the gardener, so if you add thexx coordinate of the gardener, the impact point is calculated. And place the target on the calculated x coordinate.

10. Control Direction

In this chapter, we will learn about how to use the trigonometrical function to calculate the vector size and direction. As the great Mathematician Thales calculated the height of a pyramid, which Egypt king Amasis was curious about, using the trigonometrical function, we will interpret the parabolic motion of the hammer in Garden Keeper game using the trigonometrical function.

In Garden Keeper game, if you pull the red dot representing the force, a vector box representing the size of the force appears, and in easy mode, the size and the direction of the force is displayed at the top right side. x, y axis, the force of the vector, and the angle are the contents.

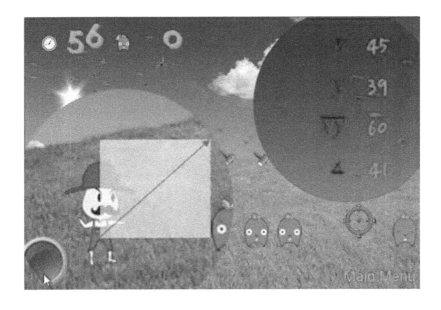

In the game, the motion direction of the hammer thrown by the gardener and the size of the force are the vector values made by the forces in x, y axis direction. How can you calculate the vector size and direction? First, we listed up the symbols composing the vector. If you set x, y axis direction vectors as $\vec{x}$ and $\vec{y}, \vec{y},$ the vector made by the two forces can be marked as $\overrightarrow{xy}$. The angle meaning the vector direction will be marked as a symbol θ.

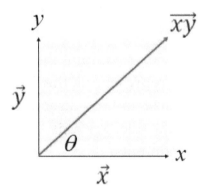

Let's list up the relationship between x, y axis direction vector $\vec{x}$ and $\vec{y}$ and vector $\overrightarrow{xy}$ made by the two forces as a formula.

$$\vec{x} + \vec{y} = \overrightarrow{xy}$$

It is a very familiar formula. Do you recall the Pythagoras' theorem which is found by Pythagoras, who is called as Father of Mathematics, as he studied the relationship of the trigonometric ratio? It is the very principle that the square of a hypotenuse of a right-angled triangle is the same as the sum of the squares of the other two sides. Since the size of x, y axis direction vector $\vec{x}$ and $\vec{y}$ of the hammer thrown by the gardener is a value that we adjust, so you can easily calculate the vector $\overrightarrow{xy}$ value which is made by the two forces.

$$a^2 + b^2 = c^2$$

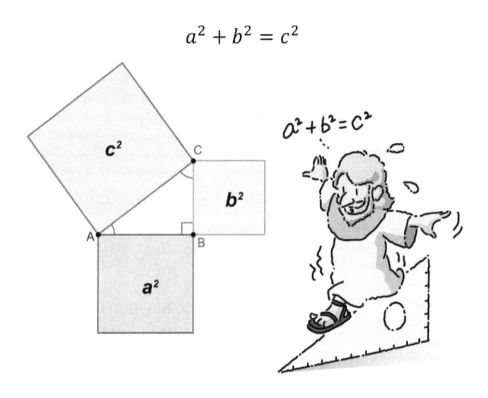

Based on the theories listed up so far, we will calculate the vector of the motion of the hammer in Garden Keeper game. x, y axis direction vector will be calculated with the name of '_deltaXvalue' and '_deltaYvalue'. And the vector $\overrightarrow{xy}$ which throws with the combination of the two vectors will be calculated with the name of 'xyVector'.

(/src/layer/GameLayer.js)

```
......

    measurePower:function( event ) {
     if( this._state == STATE_PLAYING ) {

        ......

        this._deltaXvalue = GAME.KEEPER.XPOSITION –
                        Math.round(curPos.x);
        this._deltaYvalue = GAME.KEEPER.YPOSITION –
                        Math.round(curPos.y);
        if(GAME.EASYMODE) {
          var xyVector =
                  Math.round( Math.sqrt( Math.pow(this._deltaXvalue,2) +
                  Math.pow(this._deltaYvalue,2) ));

        ......
```

This time, we will use the trigonometric function to calculate the vector $\vec{xy}$ direction angle θ. Do you remember tangent among the previously learned trigonometrical functions? In the following figure, each ∠A tangent value means the ratio of $\overline{AB}$ side and $\overline{BC}$ side.

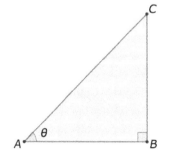

$$\tan A = \frac{\overline{BC}}{\overline{AB}}$$

If you apply the formula, formula to calculate our vector $\vec{x}$ and $\vec{y}\vec{y}$ tangent value is $\tan\theta = \vec{x} / \vec{y}$. But the value we want is not the tangent value but angle θ. To get the angle θ, we use the reverse function of tangent, which is arctangent. In such a way, you cannot use angle θ directly. It is in circular method radian value, which marks the ratio of the radius and arc as we first learned when we learned the trigonometrical function. To express it in sexadecimal system with units of degree(o) as we use, a conversion is necessary. Expression of a general formula for the relationship between the sexadecimal system angle ao and radian angle θ is as follows.

$$radian\ \theta = (\pi/180) \times a$$

Then, let's arrange the formula again based on the sexadecimal system angle ao. The sexadecimal system angle ao, which we want, can be calculated by multiplying 180 to the radian angle θ and then dividing it by π.

$$a = (radian\ \theta \times 180)/\pi$$

Now, we need to change the arranged theory into the program code. Calculate the radian angle θ of the vector $\vec{x}$ and $\vec{y}$ using the function 'Math.atan2', which calculates the arctangent, and put it in a variable named 'rad'. And, calculate the general angle by the formula to calculate the previously listed sexadecimal system degree(o) unit angle, and use it by substituting in 'degree' variable

(/src/layer/GameLayer.js)

```
......

measurePower:function( event ) {
  if( this._state == STATE_PLAYING ) {

    ......

    if(GAME.EASYMODE) {
        var rad= Math.atan2(this._deltaYvalue, this._deltaXvalue);
        var degree = Math.round( (rad*180)/Math.PI );

    ......
```

So far we learned how to use the trigonometrical function to calculate the vector and various values of parabolic motion. As we learned the principles of Mathematics and Physics, basics of the programming, and analyzed actual game program, they all do not seem so difficult. And we also found that they have a very close relationship with each other. If there is a difficult part, go back and slowly follow through, then you will see the overall picture.

I·n·d·e·x

A

B

C

D

E

J

L

M

N

O

P

R

S

W

X

Z

A Bird that flies higher
Can see farther.

The hero of the novel, 'Jonathan Livingstone Seagull'

Jonathan Livingston Seagull

A creative People
Can beautify the world.

The present writer

Jonathan Suh

Time to make Hope.

There are Hopes and dreams.
Someone still want to find their dreams.
It is time to start Your action.
Please visit the creApple web site,
www.creapple.com.
And, help someone to be great by books!

It is time to start Your action.

www.ingramcontent.com/pod-product-compliance
Lightning Source LLC
Chambersburg PA
CBHW060129060326

40690CB00018B/3804